HUMAN HORIZONS SERIES

DYSPRAXIA

Developmental and Co-ordination Disorder (DCD)

Dr Amanda Kirby

Illustrated by Sîan Koppel

A Condor Book
Souvenir Press (E&A) Ltd

First published 1999
by Souvenir Press (Educational & Academic) Ltd,
43 Great Russell Street, London WC1B 3PD

Reprinted 2000, 2001, 2002, 2003, 2004, 2005

ISBN 0 285 63512 3

Typeset by Rowland Phototypesetting Ltd, Bury St Edmunds, Suffolk
Printed in Great Britain by
Creative Print and Design Group (Wales), Ebbw Vale

Contents

Foreword

When I first wrote this book a few years ago, the term Dyspraxia was only starting to be used. Now there is greater awareness internationally. The term Dyspraxia is used by some professionals to mean one thing, but in general is used to mean a child with poor co-ordination. The term more often used today is Developmental Co-ordination Disorder or DCD. As times change labels tend to change as well. The important consistency however is practical advice to help the child and his or her family. I hope this book still remains a practical and easy to read book that can be used by professionals and parents and individuals with DCD and gives some of the answers at the differing stages of growing up.

Acknowledgements

I would like to thank Healthcall, and all the staff at the Healthcall Dyscovery Centre, without whom I could not have written this book. They have been my strength. They are just as enthusiastic about helping these very special children as I am.

I would also like to thank my long-suffering family, especially my son Andrew who has dyspraxia, without whom I would never have got involved in this area of children's health. He gave me the drive to find out what I could do to solve some of our own problems as a family, and made me feel so passionately about these children. I continue to learn a great deal from him about the deep feelings and special qualities these children have. I would also like to thank the thousands of parents I have spoken to about their own experiences as children as well as being parents of children with dyspraxia and developmental co-ordination disorder. I learn from you everyday.

Introduction

The aim of this book is to give understanding and help to parents, teachers and anyone else who comes in contact with someone who has co-ordination problems which could be dyspraxia. It describes what dyspraxia is and what you can do about it. Confirmation of a diagnosis is important to parents but for many the main issue is what can I do now? The focus of this book is to provide some of those answers.

Until recently, when the word 'dyspraxia' was mentioned, many people assumed you were talking about dyslexia. This misconception is still prevalent today. **Dyspraxia** is the name given to a condition suffered by some 'clumsy' children and affects up to one in twelve people in the population, both children and adults. It is often hidden. Children look the same as their friends but can have real problems at home and in school. The child with dyspraxia may not be able to do things like catching a ball, or his writing may be so untidy that others can't read it. Some adults still have problems and may be disorganised or find it difficult to socialise with others. They may find it hard to drive a car or do certain tasks around the house.

The diagnosis is not new and has been around for a long time but under different labels. In the past it has been called 'The Clumsy Child Syndrome', and at one time children were even referred to as 'motor morons'. Think back to your own schooldays and you will remember that there were always one or two children in the class who were bad at ball games and seemed a bit clumsy: They may well have been dyspraxic. Unfortunately, both their peer group and their teachers tended to regard them as lazy and stupid as well as clumsy. This was because of a lack of under-standing and knowledge about their difficulties.

The child with dyspraxia is often of average or above average intelligence, and with the correct help will reach his full potential. He has a specific learning difficulty. However, without help his self-esteem may take a nose-dive and he may end up feeling that it is not worth making any effort at all.

Are you a teacher? You may be a teacher who is concerned about a child in your class who seems a bit clumsy and you don't quite know what to do to help him. In this book there are some simple ideas that can be adopted in the classroom and used by all children. There may be a child who is very easily distracted and you need some strategies to cope with him. These are explained.

Are you the parent of a child who has been given the diagnosis of dyspraxia and you don't know where to turn?

The questions

You are asking, what does the future hold? At the end of the book you will find names and addresses of helpful organisations, and a glossary defining the complicated terms that may be used in your child's report by the health and educational professionals you may come across.

The early chapters in the book are written to help parents understand what they and others may feel about having a child in the family with co-ordination problems. Different chapters identify the child's difficulties from pre-school to primary school, through to the secondary school stage and on to adulthood. The pre-school chapter describes where the child's problems usually lie and gives advice on what to do about them. It also explains some of the other terms that professionals may use when assessing the child. Some difficulties described in this chapter will continue to cause problems as the individual grows up, so it would be useful to read it to gain some background understanding, even if your concerns are about an older child.

Chapter 12 addresses both the parents of a teenager and the teenager him- or herself. It looks at what problems may be experienced and offers ideas on how to resolve some of them.

The latter part of the book goes into more depth about how both dyspraxia and developmental co-ordination disorder (DCD) are diagnosed and discusses what the problem might be if it is not dyspraxia.

DCD is a term more often applied to children, some of whom are not dyspraxic, who have developmentally related co-ordination problems. The differences are explained in chapter 14. In addition, sometimes children are seen by paediatricians and neurologists and have a different problem from dyspraxia, despite having co-ordination problems. For example, they may have 'global developmental delay', affecting all aspects of development. There is more in-depth discussion about this and related issues in chapter 15. It includes some details about other specific learning difficulties, such as dyslexia and attention deficit disorder, which may overlap with dyspraxia.

It is only in the most recent years that there has been a greater understanding about dyspraxia, but it is still not known why some children have problems while others don't. It is natural for parents to want to know why it has happened to their child, even to the point of wanting to know if it was their 'fault'. Having a clear understanding of the difficulties helps them to see what to do about them. Again and again parents say, 'Don't tell me what is wrong, tell me what I can do to help my child', and very understandable this is.

Most parents would love to have a crystal ball to enable them to see what the future holds for their child. Unfortunately we can't provide that any more than we can wave a wand to magic away all the problems. Success for the child with co-ordination problems often takes longer to achieve and there may be hiccups along the way. The child may not always be able to take the traditional route, and some children may need to make several detours. That doesn't mean they won't end up having a successful adult life. The solution to the problems may not always be in the form of therapy but in understanding the right style of teaching for a particular child. At times it requires a consistent approach to see change. This may be frustrating for all concerned, including the child himself.

Realistically, all children have problems at some stage in their growing up. Like adults, they will have good and bad times. We all learn at different paces and some children learn faster than others. The pace of improvement and learning may also vary from time to time, for a variety of reasons. The child with dyspraxia will at times seem to take big steps and at times seem as if he is standing still, with no apparent progress.

The good news is that early recognition does mean earlier intervention. The first step in this process is to identify the strengths and weaknesses, and then to work on both. One of the most important keys to success for the child with co-ordination problems is maintaining self-esteem. If this can be done there is a greater chance of future success for the child, both academically and socially. He needs to have a belief in himself. The child with co-ordination problems may have experienced bullying during his school years, which will affect how he sees others around him.

The answers

The book takes a practical approach to these problems and gives solutions that may at times sound very simple. It shows parents that the answers for these children do not always lie in 'therapy'. It is not 'rocket science'—often the first steps to helping are practical, sound advice. Teaching has to be flexible to get the best from the child and the teacher may need to use whichever learning style is appropriate for the individual child rather than imposing her own style on him. This may mean taking a less conventional route to meet the child's specific needs.

To help the child improve his co-ordination, it is important to understand what else is going on in his life. Many modern parents are very busy juggling work and family. Finding time for each child under the normal stresses and strains of daily living is sometimes hard to achieve. Even harder is trying to carry out a therapy programme in addition to everything else. How much time, for example, will a mother have with three children, all under 11 years of age, to put in place any therapy programme on a regular basis. She probably has at least seven other things to do before she can even think about starting any special activity time with one child. Yet teachers and therapists often expect a weighty programme to be diligently carried out. The parent or carer then feels dispirited and guilty because she is not following the programme at all. At the same time the therapist feels disheartened and wonders why she should bother when her programme has been ignored.

Teachers and therapists need to be realistic in their expectations of parents and carers, even to the point of setting extremely simple and short activities to start with. The aim should be to try to involve the whole family. For example, a family outing going swimming can also be seen as an opportunity for the child to work on building up his shoulder strength by getting in and out of the pool or by catching and throwing a ball. Everyone else can then join in, rather than taking him away for his 'therapy'. The other children are consequently less likely to become jealous of the attention that Mum has given to their brother or sister.

Therapy or play?

If parents give 'therapy', it is often when both parent and child are too tired to enjoy a session and both parties end up getting angry and frustrated. In an ideal world therapy should be seen as child's play, but it is necessary to practise in order to become proficient at it. If the child is seeing a therapist and being given guidance, it is important to remember that one hour with the therapist or teacher each week is only one hour of treatment. There are 167 other hours that need to reinforce what has been taught. The therapist should be seen as guiding the parent and seeking active involvement from her if the best results are to be achieved. Even a short session of ten minutes per day can make a difference. The best way of helping the child is to have a partnership with health, education and the family.

If the child sees the help that is given to him as fun and not an enforced session, then he is more likely to come back for more. Remember that in school he may be pressurised to do certain tasks which he already finds difficult. He may be getting told off for not trying hard enough or not concentrating enough. If help at home is not dealt with sensitively and in a supportive environment, he could view this as being punished for his problems.

*

Finally, the book refers to the child as a male most of the time. This is not because girls do not have these problems but because at least three times the number of boys compared with girls seem to have co-ordination problems of the type described.

1 The Child and the Family

> Mothers of children with problems carry a tremendous emotional load.
> Few occupations carry as much and those that do carry a different kind.
> Fathers of neurologically handicapped children do not escape from the
> burden, but they carry it differently.
>
> (A. Jean Ayres, PhD, *Sensory Integration and the Child*)

What do parents feel when they are given the diagnosis of dyspraxia or DCD or, worse, no label at all? What effect does this have on parents or carers, not to mention the individual?

Parents are usually seen in a children's centre and a paediatrician will tell them what is wrong. If she does not give a specific label she may just describe the problem. The parents often have insufficient time to consider what questions to ask and may go away feeling mystified, not really understanding what they have been told. They may not know how to help their child and could be unaware of the implications. They may have other children and are likely to be comparing the child to them. As they leave the centre they may experience a flood of emotion and feel that they don't know what to do or where to turn. All the problems of school and home still remain to be worked out. What does it mean now? What does it mean for their child's future?

HOW DO PARENTS FEEL?

Before parents have been given a diagnosis they already know that their child is different from other children and they can see that he or she has some difficulties. When they decide to have their child 'tested' they expose themselves to a range of emotions. If you are a parent, not only of a child with co-ordination difficulties, but also

of a child who is different from the average, you may feel some of the following emotions:

Frustration. Why has it happened to me? Who should I turn to for help? I don't understand what is wrong. If only he (or she) tried harder I am sure he could ride his bike.

Anger. Why me? Why don't my friends have the same problems that we have? I feel angry with my husband; he doesn't seem to understand what I have to go through, having a child with all sorts of difficulties and trying to cope with the rest of the family. Everyone thinks I am just making it up.

Guilt. It must be something I did wrong. Maybe I didn't eat properly during the pregnancy; maybe the delivery was too fast or too slow. Perhaps it is something in my genes. Sometimes I shout at my son, and afterwards I feel that I shouldn't have, but I just can't see why he can't do some of the simplest things.

Isolation. We feel as if we are the only people in the world with a child with these problems, and nobody else seems to understand. My child looks normal, but I know he is different. I wish I could talk to someone about it.

Ignorance. What should I do to get help? Who should I turn to? There seems to be little information around.

Relief. For many parents, being given a diagnosis can bring a sense of relief. They may well have known there was something very wrong, sometimes for a long time, but didn't have a name for it. The acknowledgement of the label tells others that they were right. The name means that they can now tell other people what the problem is. It also makes it a 'real' problem, with answers to questions that may have been running around for a long time. It allows them to seek help and gain support. It says they are not being overprotective and it acknowledges and confirms their concerns. It also means they can join a support group. They are no longer alone.

Parents have to work through these feelings and understand what has happened in the past and what can be done about the problem in the years to come. Before children are born we have ideas about how we want them to be brought up and aspirations for the future. Sometimes, having these dashed is one of the hardest things to come to terms with. We then have to decide how much we should expect from our child. Many parents feel the need for guidance and a plan of action. Often, with the DCD child, small steps need to be taken, success achieved and then a plan set for the next stage in his life. A lot of the questions that are asked relate to school. Should the child stay where he is? Should he be in a special unit? Is a private school better than a state one? Many of the answers depend on the individual child, the stage of his education and the problems that he is experiencing at the time, and may need reviewing at different ages.

Ben's story
When he was seven Ben was given the diagnosis of dyspraxia by an occupational therapist. This was in contrast to other reports which had outlined his problems but had not given a diagnosis.

The occupational therapist thought that it might give the parents some hope to be told it was dyspraxia, because he did have some co-ordination problems, although there were others as well.

The diagnosis made the parents think that if they got help for the specific learning difficulty, all would then be fine with their child. In reality Ben was at least three years behind in all 'milestones' and he was also 'globally delayed' (having a low IQ). This meant that the possibilities for his future were limited.

The parents became angry when they were later told that Ben didn't have dyspraxia after all. This was not what they had expected to hear, and all they wanted was to be given some hope. Until then nobody had bothered to explain the implications for the child's learning. The label that had been given in an attempt to help had in fact not been helpful at all, but had masked the true diagnosis and the need for the parents to understand what they could realistically expect for their child.

Magic wands and quick fixes don't exist for these children, although parents always hope that there may be a 'cure' around the next corner. They need to accept that change will be slow, and at times this can seem hard when all they want is to protect their child from his problems. The DCD child needs a consistent approach to his learning, both in school and at home, if he is to reap benefits.

As in Ben's case, it happens that professionals who lack the appropriate training or qualifications may give a label of dyspraxia or DCD. The parents hear the label and assume that the child has definitely got the problem although this may not be so. Some children get misdiagnosed—they may have cerebral palsy, for example—and after years of coming to terms with the first diagnosis the parents may have to adjust to the new one. This can be particularly hard to cope with.

The child with co-ordination difficulties will have an impact on the whole family and at times may limit their activities. For example, if one child cannot ride a bike then the whole family cannot go out for a bike ride together. The child with feeding and social difficulties can also limit outings and contact with other families. Going out to a restaurant can be embarrassing if the child ends up spilling food everywhere. Parents sometimes even feel angry with their child and end up preferring to stay at home, away from other people. Criticism from others, even the odd frown, can be painful if you already feel sensitive about the situation.

Tension can also rise *between* the parents of the child when there is a lack of understanding or support. Some fathers may have seen their child as a potential rugby star, and when these hopes are dashed because the child can't even catch or throw well, disappointment, anger and frustration may creep in but not be openly discussed. The father may not have been able to attend hospital or school appointments and may not have the same understanding as the mother. He may feel ignorant about his child's difficulties.

Problems may be highlighted even more when another sibling comes along. This younger child may reach milestones, such as walking and talking, at a much faster rate. The child may then pass the other one in some skills and this accentuates the magnitude of the problem. This gap may widen as the children get older.

What can you do as a parent?

✓ If you think there is a problem with your child, ask for help. If you don't get it at first you may need to keep asking. Is there a local Dyspraxia Foundation support group in your area? Meet other parents who may have experienced similar problems and found answers. If there isn't a group near you, consider starting one—you could just ask a few parents round for a cup of coffee and a chat. Ask the teacher in your child's school if she knows of any other parents who have children with similar problems.

✓ Join another support organisation, like Afasic or the British Dyslexia Association, if there isn't one for dyspraxia in your area. The parents will have had similar problems and experiences and will provide support and information.

✓ Talk to other people. You will be surprised what you can find out, and remember, you are an expert too. You will have found ways round problems which will also help others.

✓ Read about the problem, knowledge is very powerful. Look on the Internet, go to the library, and ask the therapist who sees your child if she can recommend some books or leaflets. Also ask your child's teacher how much she knows.

✓ Give out information to others—you may help other parents.

✓ Talk to each other, parent to parent. Feelings of frustration can get bottled up inside and just surface as anger. You may not have talked to each other about how you feel and may both be feeling inadequate in different ways.

✓   Seek help for your child. You will then feel more in control
     of the situation.
✓   If there are professional health and education meetings in
     your area, consider going along. This is also a good way of
     networking, and you may find out the latest information and
     research into the problems. You can always ask questions if
     you don't understand it all at the time

WHAT ABOUT THE CHILD HIMSELF?

How much does your child know about his problem? Have you
ever discussed it with him? Parents often feel that they shouldn't
talk about this with their children as it may make it worse for
them. How much should your child know? What should he tell
other children if he is called names? What is the best way of
equipping him?

By the age of six the child with dyspraxia will already have a
clear idea that he has problems and is different from other children. He can see that he can't achieve the same things at the same
pace as his peer group—he may not be able to ride a bike, or
his handwriting may look different from other children's. Even
worse, he may see that he is not invited to other children's parties,
for example, and feel both frustrated and angry. One child of six,
who was seen at a specialist centre, said that all he wanted was to
be dead. He had even thought about how he might kill himself,
and his emotions were very real.

Sometimes as parents we do not allow children to show how
they feel and unknowingly encourage them to remain bottled up.
It is thought wrong for them to be angry or upset, even though we
as adults show these emotions. Children, like adults, need explanation and support. For example, the child's behaviour may be
fine in school, and he may seem to be able to hold himself
together very well. Teachers may tell his parents that he sits very
quietly at the back of the class, not joining in very much but not
being disruptive. The parents cannot believe this is the same child
who, when he gets home every night, is loud and quarrelsome,
even physically aggressive towards other family members. The
child sees home as his safe haven and knows that, whatever
behaviour he displays, at the end of the day his parents will still
love him. This is why he shows his frustrations at home. Of
course this can be very exhausting for the parents!

Your child may well have been bullied and you may need to deal with this as well. It may be manifested physically, by shoves and pushes in the playground, or verbally, by attacking the way he looks or acts. This is very wounding for a child who is trying to sort out who he is. He is also seeking friendship and wants reassurance from his peer group. (See chapters 8 and 11 for advice on dealing with this.)

Tips to help

✓ Talk to your child and explain that he is different, but so is everyone else in some way. He needs to know and feel special about himself. He needs to see that there are solutions to his problems.

✓ Allow him to come and tell you when things are not going right, and let him see that you believe him.

✓ He cannot use his problems as an excuse for bad behaviour. Accept his feelings but also tell him you don't always accept his actions if they are inappropriate.

✓ Explain to others about his problems so that they give him a chance and are a little more patient with him.

✓ If possible, let your child meet other children with similar problems so that he doesn't feel he is the only one.

✓ He could have a pen or tape pal.

BROTHERS AND SISTERS

What does it feel like to be the brother or sister of a child with dyspraxia or DCD? Is there the same sibling rivalry that is seen in every family or is it different for these children?

Having a child in the family with co-ordination difficulties can have a profound and unsettling effect on the siblings. They have a range of emotions that they have to deal with themselves. Parents may not even have discussed what the problem is with their brother or sister, or they may have done so only in hushed tones. However, they see that their parents need to spend more time with their brother or sister and they may become resentful of this.

What do the siblings feel?

Anger. Why do *we* have a brother or sister with a problem? It stops me doing the things that *I* want to do. We can't all go out for a bike ride when we want to. He always seems to be getting more time and attention from Mum and Dad than I do.

Sympathy. I feel sorry for my brother, he seems to try hard but never has any friends. I get asked out to parties and he seems to be at home all the time. He's so clumsy, he is always spilling things all over himself. If only I could help him, but I don't know what to do.

Ignorance. What is dyspraxia? No one has explained it to me at all. He just seems to be a pain. If I understood then perhaps I could help, at least I would know why he has these problems.

Support. I make sure he's OK in school. The other kids go after him in the playground and call him names. I hang around, as I'm bigger, and threaten them if they touch him. I do worry about him, though.

Embarrassment. I can't believe how he behaves when he's with my friends. He acts the fool. He spills everything when we're out. I just wish he would go out when my friends come round. The other day he came in with his trousers down to ask Mum to wipe his bottom!

Tips to help the siblings

✓ 'Ring-fence' times for all your children. Whether it is a short time each day or once a week, give them each a set time. Whatever times you choose, stick to them.

✓ Let their class teacher know they have a sibling with diffi-culties. It may affect them at school if their brother or sister is having problems.

✓ The support group may organise parties where siblings can

also go. Bring them along, so that they can see they are not the only ones.

✓ When they have friends round, try to make sure they have their own space and, if you can, occupy their brother or sister so that he or she doesn't embarrass them. They still need their own space at times.

✓ Try to do activities that can involve the whole family — for example, bowling, badminton, swimming, going for a walk, going to the cinema, rather than one that excludes part of the family.

✓ If you can, let each child have a hobby that is different from the others so that there are no comparisons.

QUESTIONS YOU MAY ASK

Why me?

Well, it could be anybody. DCD does seem to run in some families and, as previously stated, affects three times as many boys as girls. Some children also seem to have a family history of dyslexia.

Did I do something that I shouldn't have done while I was pregnant?

So far we haven't seen any link between pregnancy and this type of problem, but this requires further research.

Is it because I didn't give him enough attention when he was a baby?

No. Most parents have usually been very attentive. However, as your child has a problem you may need to play certain games or do some exercises to help him.

I had post-natal depression. Is this why he didn't develop properly?

No. When you are depressed, you often feel guilty about the things that you should be doing, and you may feel that you didn't give your child much attention. If you feel depressed now, so long as there are others to care for him and stimulate him, he should be fine. As you get better you will once again enjoy playing and being with your child. If you are worried about this, talk to your GP or psychiatrist who may be able to offer some additional help.

Should I have another child?

Although, as we know, it does seem to run in some families, in most cases it should not stop you having other children. You will be more alert to the problems and how you can help and approach your child to make sure he or she is supported in school and at home. There are some genetic disorders, like Duchenne Muscular Dystrophy, which may also cause co-ordination problems. If your child had this you would usually be offered specialist counselling.

What help is available?

Help is available in various forms and is described in this book. If you suspect your child has dyspraxia or DCD, go and talk to your GP, health visitor or the schoolteacher. Find out if there is a support group in your area (see Directory of Resources). Your child may be able to get a disability living allowance or other help, and there are organisations that will help you with this.

What happens if he needs an assessment?

This depends on what his problems are. He may be seen by an educational psychologist, an occupational therapist, physiotherapist, speech and language therapist, behavioural optometrist or a paediatrician or neurologist. They will decide if your child has a specific problem and what help he requires. It will also be decided if he needs a statement of educational need or an individual educational plan (IEP) for school and in what form this help will be given.

What happens if my child needs treatment?

This may be done on his own, or in a group. Treatment is sometimes given in blocks of several weeks, followed by a break—a bit like school with holidays. It does depend on the provision of services in your area and will vary considerably.

Will treatment 'cure' my child?

Some problems get better with help and some stay the same despite help. Treatment may help your child cope with the problem better and find ways around it, rather than getting rid of all the problems. Treatment only represents a small part of the child's week. For it to be successful it needs to be backed up by practice sessions in between. Therapy may teach new skills which he lacks, teach him to compensate for things he finds difficult, and will sometimes teach him how to live with his difficulties.

What can I do?
Learn as much as possible about the educational system in your area, looking at both the independent and state sector for schooling depending on the needs of your child. Where you live also affects what provision there is for therapy. Learn about DCD and how this fits in to your child's problems. Don't blame yourself. Give yourself time to understand *what* is wrong, and be realistic about what *can* be done. **You are your child's expert and know more about him or her than anyone else, so remember that**. If you don't get the help you need, keep trying. Don't give up and don't lose heart. You may feel very alone at times, but remember there are lots of other parents in the same boat.

Why is it other families don't have these problems?
There isn't a family without some problems. They are all different. Struggling with kids growing up is hard to do whatever the problem. Looking after the DCD child is even more challenging. You do need to remember to take some time for yourself as well. You can get burnt out and be unable to give your best to your child, the rest of the family or yourself. Talk to friends and make sure you have some time to relax.

Is dyspraxia something I should have recognised?
There is no reason why you should. The health and education profession still knows little about it, and that is why we see children failing in school before they are identified.

Why don't other people understand his behaviour?
That's the hard thing about these problems. Your child looks the same as other children, but he may act differently at times. These children can be emotionally very young for their age and not cope well under pressure. They may show this by having a tantrum and this can be embarrassing for the whole family, as well as others. Try to talk to your friends and they will start to understand your own frustrations and to see that your child is actually trying to do his best.

Will he grow out of it?

Many children find that their co-ordination improves as they get older. They also no longer have to do things they had to do in school—for example, you don't have to play rugby when you are an adult. You can also learn splinter skills to let you achieve certain things. Splinter skills are those skills that allow you to do a particular task in certain circumstances. The child may not be able to transfer this skill—for example, he may manage to tie his shoelaces but be unable to tie a bow behind him. There is usually an answer to most problems; sometimes you have to find a different way of getting around them or learn to use different tools to do the job.

When will be the worst time for children like mine?

This is probably between the ages of 7 and 15. By the time they are between six and seven many children have some insight into their problems and realise they are different from other children. Moving from infants to juniors and from primary to secondary school increases the pressure on the child to perform. Children are also supposed to join in all activities, with little choice. They cannot choose the ones that they find easier.

Is there any medicine he can take to help?

There is no medicine at the moment that will 'cure' the problem. Some people have tried evening primrose oil products, and have seen some improvement. However, there have been no large trials to prove whether they work and it is not known if they are useful for all children with co-ordination difficulties. There are different subgroups within the DCD grouping, and it is possible that there may be a need for different treatments for each of these groups. We don't know this as yet.

Should I tell other people he has a problem?

This is always difficult. It is often better to let people know that your child has difficulties in some areas, but also take the opportunity to talk about your child's strengths. It will allow the teacher or cub pack-leader, for example, to be patient with your child and perhaps give him extra time to complete work or approach an activity in a different way.

Why is it he can sometimes do some things but not others?
This is hard to explain. It may be to do with fatigue. These children have to concentrate much harder to achieve anything and by the end of most days they are very tired. He may also seem to have 'off' times when he finds it harder to take in new concepts and concentrate on his work. He needs to be given a chance to consolidate his skills. Be patient. He may sometimes seem to learn in steps rather than in a gradual smooth upward gradient.

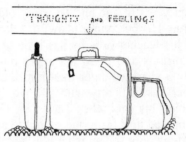

THOUGHTS AND FEELINGS

Some parents' thoughts

'I wanted my child to be seen and diagnosed but my husband has said that I am the problem and that he doesn't want his son to be given the diagnosis of dyspraxia. He has said that I need to sort myself out. I know my boy has problems. He has real difficulty with his writing and he can't make friends very well. I only want to get the best help for him. Even the paediatrician says he has a problem. My husband disagrees. I don't know what to do.'

'Parenting of "normal" children is hard enough, but parenting of my child is even tougher. Last week I felt emotionally drained and exhausted. The only thing that I found would calm my son was to hold him tight and squeeze him hard.'

'I sometimes don't know what I am going to do. We have moved him from school to school because he finds it hard to make friends. All I want is that he should be happy. I must have explained so many times to the teachers what is wrong, but they still don't seem to understand. They stuck his work on the wall the other day and even he knew it looked awful. Why couldn't they see that and type it out or write it for him? I don't know where he will end up. He is so angry at times with everyone and most of all with himself. I often feel at a loss to know how to help him and where to turn for help. The other day I met another mother and I just knew she understood.

'Sometimes I am looked on as a fussy mother. I do know how bright he is and how he has to fight all the way. I get desperate for help. The good teachers he has had have been brilliant and let him enjoy their teaching. I need to know whether he will cope when he gets older and if he'll be able to get a job.'

'My son is seven years of age and he is my oldest child. I have two other children. His behaviour is awful. I don't know what to do. I hear from his teacher how he has hit a child in school. At home he has tantrums and takes his anger out on his younger brother. He is two years younger than him, but can already do things his brother has difficulty with. He won't talk to me and puts his hands over his ears when I ask him to tell me how he feels. We have moved him from one school to another to try and get some help. He is only seven, what will happen later on when he's older?

'He doesn't have many friends. If he does ask children to play, he wants them to do what he wants and gets angry with them when they won't. He then walks off. When we had seen a doctor who told us he had dyspraxia, he came home and sat on his bed and started to cry and said, "Am I going to die, Mummy?" All I wanted to do was cry with him. How can I help him, when I don't know what to do myself?'

'We became aware that something was not right at an early age, but this was initially put down to his being a lazy boy, having had two bright girls. Although generally a warm and giving child, frustration showed through. How would he cope with life in the future, and leaving home?'

A thirteen-year-old boy

'It's not fair that I have problems. I don't mean to get it wrong, I am trying my hardest. The teachers don't understand and they keep shouting at me and the boys call me "Spastic"! I have told them I am not because I know what that is, and they just tell me to shut up. I got into trouble the other day because I showed this spider to a boy who was frightened of them. I thought the others would laugh with me, but I got told off instead. I just didn't think. They all said I was stupid. Sometimes I want Mum to teach me at home and get a tutor for me, because they call me names. I know I am clever but it's hard to show everyone else.'

Adult who has co-ordination problems and is a parent of a child with them

'I am now 45 years old, and my son has been diagnosed with co-ordination problems. Looking at him I now realise that I have had the same problems as him all my life. My mother said that I was just stupid and that not to consider a career and I should just get married as early as possible. At eight years of age I tried to kill myself. I lifted a metal bed and tried to drop it on my neck I was so unhappy. I am now studying through Open University to get a Psychology degree and I just won't let the same thing happen to my child that happened to me. My mother still won't admit that I had a problem and I feel very angry with her.'

An adult reflecting on his childhood

'Playtime was my favourite in school. At junior school I knew I couldn't keep up with the rest. I was bullied. Fortunately my grandfather taught me how to fight. Staff ridiculed me. For years I thought, "If I can't do this I must be stupid." There was a great rift between myself and my family, my feelings of isolation and loneliness grew ever more difficult to deal with. I felt I belonged nowhere and with no one, totally alone and worthless. My sister was doing 'A' levels and going to university. You develop ways of surviving . . .

'Today I am at peace with myself but it took many years.'

A father

'All I wanted for my son was that he would play football with me, after having two daughters. I know with a bit of practice he would be able to do it. He just doesn't want to. When he comes home from school all he wants to do is slump in front of the television. If he just tried a bit harder he'd be all right. His mother says he's bullied and she gets very worried about him. We all have problems and he should just put up with it and he'd grow out of it. I feel frustrated sometimes that he won't try and seems to give up too easily. Even the things he can do well he doesn't want to try at. I love him but I do feel I don't know what to do at times with him.'

A teacher

'I just don't understand why she's better in the morning than the afternoon. She can sometimes do some really good work and then it all goes to pot! I think if she concentrated a bit more she would be fine. She is very fidgety. Always wriggling in her seat. She even manages to fall off it at times. She seems to knock into everyone as she goes around the class. Every week she has lost another ruler or her pencils, and she always seems to leave a book at home. I don't know whether she is doing this on purpose or really forgetting.'

A younger sister

'Why is it that Mum gives my brother so much more time than me? He isn't even well behaved. He's always such a mess and lies around doing nothing. When I have friends over he plays the fool and I am so embarrassed I don't want him there. I have to explain to them why he is like that.

'He punches me sometimes; even when I haven't done anything. He stops us all going out together. I like riding my bike and he can't ride a bike, so we can't all go on the bike trail together. He is so revolting sometimes when he eats, it all goes everywhere. I love him a lot but sometimes he really annoys me and goes on and on.'

A friend of an eleven-year-old boy

'I like him, but sometimes he can be a pain. He doesn't always want to play with the same things as me, and then he goes off in a strop. I know he can't play football very well, but we take the dogs out for a walk instead. We also like playing on the computer. We'll do that for ages. The one thing he likes is the television and when he watches that he doesn't want to play a game. He likes me to come round and we go bowling together.'

2   The Pre-school Child

It is well understood that children develop at different rates. One child arriving at nursery school will be able to recognise his name, or to speed competently around on a tricycle, while another will be just out of nappies.

Children often develop in spurts and may gain some skills quickly and then plateau off for a while before apparently learning again. They may hit the developmental milestones at differing rates.

If you watch children in a nursery-school setting, you may well see widely varying behaviour. Little girls with powers of great concentration sit at a table doing their colouring-in, and little boys of the same age may be seen running all over the place, unable to concentrate for more than five minutes at a time. Even though the variation is great at this stage, there will be signs suggesting that some children are more delayed in certain areas than one would expect. When these are noticed, action should be taken to give the children a chance to catch up with their peer group. Early

recognition can remediate many of the problems for these children.

We know that developmental milestones—the times when children do certain things like crawling, walking, and talking—are not set in stone, but for some children the time taken to acquire these skills seems to be greater than you would expect compared to the average child.

Variation may be due to:

The child's environment. The child may not have been exposed to using a knife and fork, or have practised colouring or cutting. He needs time to catch up.

Family position. The first child has one-to-one attention, and high expectations to do things all in the right order and at the 'correct' time. She may be cajoled to move on and do the next thing—for example, by putting her in the crawling position ready to crawl. The second child may be allowed to develop at his own pace.

Sex. Boys are sometimes slower in a family, reaching some milestones later than their sisters. In some cases the elder sibling may be the one doing the talking for them, for example.

Genetic. Families as a whole achieve certain milestones at different times. In one family all the children seem to walk by a year, but in another it may be later.

Language. A child learning to speak two languages may take longer to start talking, while he is absorbing the knowledge required to do so.

Social. Society's expectation will vary from one setting to another. In some societies the child will go through 'potty-training' from a few months of age onwards; in other social groups the child wouldn't be started before he is 2½ years old. Reading in some Scandinavian countries, for example, does not start until the age of six or seven. Contrast this with the UK where children are

sent to school at four and taught to read. The expectation for them is to be ready to do this at an earlier age.

Cultural. In some cultures, from a young age the child will be carried around by his mother. This will continue for longer, and he may not be given the opportunity to explore his environment.

Welcome to our nursery

What may be different in the child with dyspraxia and related problems?

At pre-school age detecting differences between children can be quite difficult. It may mean observing a child over a period of time and seeing if there is a pattern of difficulty or delay.

Questions to ask
- Is the child delayed in all areas of development or just in specific areas, such as those related to co-ordination? This is the difference between global delay and specific learning difficulties.
- At what pace is the child developing—normally along all lines, but just more slowly?
- Are there other specific learning difficulties in the family—a sibling with dyslexia or ADHD?
- Was the child late walking and talking, and did he crawl? Has he suffered from recurrent ear infections like glue ear or otitis media, and has he still got hearing problems? Is he epileptic? Has he been unwell at a crucial stage in his development?
- Has the child any other reason for the delay—could he have cerebral palsy or muscular dystrophy?

- Can he stand on one leg unaided, or kick a ball?
- How does he hold a pen? Has he established later-ality—using one hand for writing and cutting most of the time—or does he swap from side to side?
- How does he sit at story time—can he sit still or does he fidget and wander off?
- What is his attention-span like—is he easily distracted?

After a period of observation and intervention in a nursery school, if the problem was lack of previous exposure the child should have caught up with his peers. This is unlike the child with co-ordination difficulties who will take longer to acquire the skills, even if he has been previously exposed to them. This is an important distinction.

DIFFICULTIES YOU MAY IDENTIFY
(see Glossary for definitions)

- Fine motor problems
- Gross motor problems
- No laterality and lack of bilateral integration
- Visual perceptual difficulties
- Auditory perceptual difficulties
- Poor body awareness (kinaesthesia)
- Poor propioception

Fine motor control

This is the small movements we make with our hands that require dexterity. Children need to be able to move their fingers independently and also to be able to oppose their thumb with their other

fingers. The first stage in this process is to be able to pick up a raisin or other similar small object in a pincer grasp, which we would expect by the age of nine months. A pincer grasp is when the finger and thumb can oppose each other. Without good fine motor control children have difficulty with eating, dressing, writing, cutting and colouring.

✓   Practise threading and buttoning (see chapter 3 for further ideas).

Tripod grip
The child may not have developed a tripod grip—that is, holding a pencil with the web space open between the finger and thumb and maintaining the position.

Handwriting
This may be very crude and the child may have an inability to write on a line or colour in between lines.

✓   Start big and work small. Improving shoulder stability may help the child's fine motor skills. Consider working on the child's gross motor skills first.
✓   Use big sheets of paper and big pens and brushes which will be easier, but give your child a choice of tools to use.

Cutting
He may find it hard to use scissors—to place his fingers in the holes and to co-ordinate the 'open and close' movement required to cut. He may also be unable to hold a piece of paper in the other hand to manipulate the two objects (see exercises for scissor skills on pp. 72–6).

Gross motor function

This is the large movements that allow us to balance and walk and run and catch and throw a ball. If a child has poor balance he will find it difficult to carry out these tasks. He may have low tone and therefore be floppier. This is why it is harder for him to remain upright and may require more effort and attention than for other children.

If he is knocked into by other children he will be unable to right himself sufficiently quickly and may end up falling over or bumping into objects around him.

✓ Work on shoulder and hip strength as much as possible to increase the stability of the child. The more stable he is, the better his hand and foot function will be. Think about a crane—the steadier it is, the easier it is to pick up objects.

Poor gross motor skills affect the following areas:

Ball skills
The child with DCD will find it hard to make some of the big movements because of his instability. If he is trying to stand up and also catch a ball, this may be too much for him. He may show

a 'blink response' when a ball is thrown at him or even turn away from the ball rather than try to catch it. He may even throw his arms out rather than putting his hands together. If the child cannot use both sides of his body he may turn and try to catch unevenly and lose stability as well.

Kicking a ball may be difficult, and also aiming it accurately. The child may kick too hard or too soft rather than learning from his errors and the next time adjusting the power of his kick. He often has problems grading his movements.

✓　Start with a big ball made of foam that moves more slowly. Sit the child down and pass the ball back and forth between his legs. Use balloons to throw and catch. They move more slowly and give him time to guess where they will fall. Use a slow-moving object at a big target, which gives a greater chance of success.

✓　Use big bats and big balls, or a ball with a large target area, like a football goal. Success will make him want to keep going.

Crawling, running and rolling and standing on one leg
These may also be a problem. Standing on one leg requires stability in the supporting leg and the hip. You may see the child wobbling all over the place, as well as moving his arms, and he may even make mouthing movements to try to compensate for his instability.

✓　Let him practise commando crawling (crawling on his tummy), wheelbarrow races (arms down and legs held up by another person) and swimming to improve his gross motor function.

Walking downstairs or along a wall
The child will often be better at climbing up the stairs than down and may show fear when going down. He may walk downstairs one foot at a time rather than using alternate feet. This will continue after the stage where others would have gained the necessary skills and confidence. Other children usually enjoy walking along a wall, while this child will be fearful and need a great deal of support while doing it. You may see a similar response when he is climbing on a climbing frame.

Part of the problem may be due to **visual perceptual problems**. This can affect the child in the following way. Imagine what it is like to walk around with one eye shut and one eye open: you lose your judgement regarding depth; you see things in a 2D way. These children often have a depth perception problem like this, so that when they walk downstairs they cannot judge how deep the steps are. They will have to test each one every time. As an adult we can run downstairs carrying objects and holding a conversation. This would be almost impossible for some children with DCD to do.

✓   Try to see if he can walk along a line marked out on the floor and see how he walks downstairs. If this is a problem you may need to consider taking him to see a behavioural optometrist.

Experience what it feels like:
Take a pair of binoculars and reverse them round the 'wrong' way. Now try to walk round objects in your home or at school. What does this feel like? Do you feel confident about what you are doing? Now try to walk up and down the stairs and compare the difference. This uncertainty about their surroundings is something these children have to face all the time.

Bilateral integration

Because of delayed development these children may not be able to integrate both sides of their body. They need to be able to do this in order to use a knife and fork or to draw or ride a bike. The skill requires the child to stabilise himself with one hand and write with the other. Even crawling and walking require him to use both sides of his body. Consequently, riding a tricycle may be hard to achieve.

Laterality

Some children not have developed laterality. They may not be
good with either hand. They may be seen to write with one hand
and then use a fork with the other, and this too may vary from
time to time.

✓   Give them the opportunity to practise, but make sure the
     tools are appropriate—for example, left-handed and right-
     handed scissors.
✓   Start with 'chunky' crayons and pencils. They may need to
     use pencil grips or require the barrel of the pen to be made
     fatter, using foam tubing.

Visual discrimination

This means that 'busy' walls, with paintings and drawings, combined with the movement of the other children around the classroom, may distract the child from the task that he is trying to
achieve or which has been set for him. The nursery setting is often
one where the walls are covered in work, and this may make it
harder for the child to concentrate.

Visual perceptual difficulties
Some children will not be able to discriminate one shape from
another, or feel confident about how deep something is. They will
not be able to see, for example, that a jigsaw piece turned one way
is the same piece when turned round—that a triangle is still the
same triangle whichever way you look at it.

✓   Start with simple puzzles which require the child to place
     just one or two pieces into the pattern, and gradually build
     up from this.
✓   Speak to your child as you play with him to practise the
     meanings of the 'small words'—on, top, bottom, up, down,
     etc. In the kitchen you can talk about size—for example, the
     bigger and smaller pans.
✓   Dot-to-dot games are useful to do.

Auditory discrimination

The child may not be able to filter out unnecessary sounds. You
may see him constantly turning round and looking out of the win-

dows. He may say to you that he has heard a train going by, or a bell going in the corridor. Other children seem to be able to filter out the extraneous sounds and decide which are the most important ones — for example, in the nursery setting they would be able to listen to the teacher telling a story. A child who has dyspraxia may find this very difficult and feel he is being bombarded by sounds.

✓   He may respond far better in a quiet setting.
✓   At times in the nursery, if this is possible, he may benefit from doing some activities in a quiet area, away from the other children.

Poor body awareness (kinaesthesia)

The child is not aware that he is a 3D object with a front and a back. If you look at how children draw human figures at this stage, you will see that they have arms sticking out of their heads! They are not very stable either. However, if you can understand that they are unaware of where their arms are, you can then see why they tend to bump into doors and tables as they walk around. The child won't know how near his hand is to an object because he is unaware of where his body is at any one time. He will need to use his vision more to check this out. It is little surprise, then, that the child has problems wiping his bottom when it is 'somewhere behind him'!

Poor proprioception

Proprioception derives from the Latin meaning 'one's own'. This is the sensations received from the muscles and joints. Proprioceptive input tells the brain when and how the joints are bending, extending or being pulled or compressed. This information enables the brain to know where each part of the body is and how it is moving. The dyspraxic child may have poor feedback and cannot then readjust his movements properly to correct errors he is making. For example, if a child without co-ordination problem throws a ball too hard and too far, the next time he will try to throw more gently to reach his target. The child with dyspraxia and related problems may not be able to do this as well. The feedback messages he gives to his brain don't seem to be as good as those of other children. You may see him stamping his feet when he is walking along, to make sure there are more definite messages returning. He doesn't realise he is doing this, but has learnt that this is the best way to know where he is and what he is doing.

Change

All children like to know what they are doing and where they are going. This makes them feel more confident. The child with co-ordination difficulties does not usually respond well to change. He needs plenty of time to prepare for this. Often his concept of time is poor, and so if you say to him 'we are going out in five minutes', when you come to fetch him you may find him still sitting at the end of the bed, staring out of the window. He will find repetition and a clear timetable reassuring and he will work better in a structured environment.

✓ Write down what you will be doing with your child. For the younger child who cannot read you could make a series of picture cards that he can have with him, so he can see what will be happening through the day. You can then *say* as well as *show* him what you will be doing.

Sequencing

Some children have a problem with sequencing, so when they are given a series of commands or instructions they will only remember the last one said. They may have difficulty learning times tables or placing their clothes in the correct order to put them on.

SOCIAL SKILLS

The pre-school child may tend to watch the other children around him, rather than joining in the games they are playing. To enjoy a social existence you need confidence, an understanding of the rules of when to start and when to stop, and you need to know how to make friends and then what to talk about. Many of these skills normally 'come naturally', as opposed to being taught. The DCD child seems not to have absorbed some of these rules and has not learnt them intuitively. We are often unaware how much these skills are 'absorbed' rather than taught.

The child wants to socialise but can't understand why he is being rebuffed. He may run into the other children or shout too loud. He may also interrupt when the others are talking. He finds it harder to learn the social skills that the other children are learning by absorption and needs to be shown exactly what to do. Unlike the autistic child, he *does want* to join in and be sociable, but when he tries he gets it wrong. He may approach a child in the nursery setting and sit down too close to him or give too much (staring) or too little eye contact. Other children, even at a young age, are quick to recognise the differences and the DCD child will be alienated even at this early stage.

The child may be having great difficulty just concentrating and maintaining this for any period of time while he is at nursery. Trying to socialise at the same time is sometimes too much for him.

✓   Give him opportunities to use his language skills. Let him describe his morning or afternoon session at nursery. Take him to the park or go swimming with him alongside other children. Invite and encourage other children to come to your house. It will be easier for him to practise in a one-to-one situation rather than with a group.

✓   If he behaves inappropriately or gets overexcited, guide him out of the situation. If necessary take him out of the room for a few minutes to let him calm down. He may not know how to do so.

Signs of frustration and anger

Some children may show their frustration by attacking those closest to them. For the child the parent is seen as 'safe' and will still be there the following day, despite what has gone on at home. The child with co-ordination problems is typically well behaved at this age. He may appear quiet and withdrawn in school but may not be good at relating to his peers. He has to concentrate so hard to join in and keep up that he often appears exhausted by the time he gets home. By nursery school, most children will only have the occasional tantrum, but this child may still continue them for quite some time whenever he feels under pressure. It is harder for him at this stage to say what is wrong in words, and he will tend to act this out with his negative behaviour to his parents, with whom he feels most secure.

Emotion

The child with dyspraxia may act more like a younger child, wanting frequent attention and reassurance from the adults around him to give him the help and support he feels he needs. His verbal skills are usually better than his performance skills—he may be able to carry on a reasonable conversation, but be unable to complete a simple task.

In a group situation the child may not be able to react at the same speed as the other children. He may be inclined to opt out, because by the time he has got his answer ready the group has moved on. At times he may seem inattentive or fidgety.

For the low-toned child the act of sitting in a circle on the floor, or trying to keep balanced on a chair, is hard enough. In addition to this, trying to listen to a story and perhaps being knocked into by other children may sometimes seem just too much. The appearance of a fidgety and inattentive child may be due to insta-bility, but he could be wrongly labelled as having attention deficit disorder (ADD).

The child may get up and want to wander around. It may be his only way of dealing with this situation. Each time he has to change his position on the floor he has to do so consciously. For other chil-dren this is done subconsciously and they do not have to use up all their attention just to keep themselves on the floor or balanced on a chair. They can use this attention more appropriately on the tasks they are being asked to do, such as listening to a story.

✓   Give the child time to talk about his feelings. At this age he may need to let off steam when he gets home from nursery, to get rid of his feelings of frustration.

✓   See how he sits on the floor. Does he sit up straight or is he curled and looking uncomfortable? Try 'propping' him against a wall or sit him on a low chair.

HELPFUL HINTS FOR NURSERY SCHOOL

Seating

Make sure the child is sitting comfortably on a chair which is the correct height for him. Ensure that his feet are on the floor and his hips and knees at 90 degrees. If he is on the floor:

✓ He may need to prop himself with his back against a wall rather than sit freely. Try not to sit him too close to the other children. The movement and touch may be enough to unbalance him.

✓ He may feel safer nearer to the teacher, and may even respond to an arm around him to make him feel more secure.

Communication

✓ Give the child some time one-to-one, when he can talk to you at his own pace. For the child the speed of conversations and the type of words used, even at this age, may feel like listening to someone speaking to him in another language. He may not understand the nuances of the language. Missing out the 'nots' and the 'no's' can change the meaning of the sentences. He may see things very literally—for example, 'pull up your socks' may prompt him to do just that, not realising that it means to try harder.

✓ On days when he seems to be 'switched off', allow the child to play at his own pace and do not push him too hard.

Giving instructions

✓ Use visual instructions as well as verbal commands to help the child understand. Show him and tell him what you expect him to do.

✓ Give instructions in instalments so that he can cope with and understand what is being asked of him. Don't give a long string of instructions, he will not be able to recall them and will feel both confused and frustrated.

✓ Start at the end, not the beginning. If you are teaching him a new skill, such as tying shoelaces, start at the end so that he just has to finish the last bit. He then sees success rather than feeling frustrated by his inability.

✓ Gain the child's attention before giving the command. You may need to touch him on the shoulder and say his name. If you touch him, make sure you do so firmly, as a light touch may be confusing and give him poor feedback messages, and he may jump or startle.

Coping with time and change

✓ Allow the child time to calm down after an activity. This may take longer than with other children of a similar age.
✓ Prepare him in advance for any changes that may occur. For example, when going on a school outing, talk to him about it for a few days before you go, and explain where you will be going and what you will be doing, even if it is only to a local park.
✓ Give him a structured environment and a timetable to follow—this could be in a pictorial version for the younger child. He could make this with you, cutting out pictures, for example.
✓ Use an egg-timer as a reminder, to let him know when a certain time is up.
✓ Let him improve his sequencing skills by cutting up a series of pictures and getting him to order them first and then to tell the story—which comes first, second and so on. Encourage him to use language that describes this. Talk about this in other settings, too. For example, at drink time say, 'Who do you start with? Now who is next?'
✓ Try to get the child to talk 'through' a puppet or toy. He may be more ready to tell you how he is feeling if you do this. Finger puppets are also good for improving fine motor control skills.

Promoting language skills

The child may have a specific language problem. This can be at the ear level, the brain level or the output level in the form of speech. He may have had 'glue ear', which has affected his hearing intermittently. Or it may be a higher-level problem in which the brain may not be able to decode the messages it is hearing. The teacher sometimes sees the child as one who is 'hearing but not understanding'. Lastly, the problem could be at the output stage, in the way he produces language. He may have dribbled excessively as a baby and may still do this now. He may produce 'sloppy' speech, in which the sounds are still indistinct. This problem may even become worse when he is tired or unwell.

✓ Talk to the child and take him out walking in the park, to the zoo or a museum where he has an opportunity to talk about his environment.

✓ Use language in play: 'Put the book *on* the table, now *under* the table, climb *through* the tunnel.'

✓ Sing songs to him that help him with sounds and the rhythm of language—for example, 'Baa baa, black sheep', where he can join in—and marching games with rhythm, such as 'The Grand Old Duke of York'.

✓ Play matching the object to the sound—blindfold him and let him guess first where the sound is coming from and then what the sound is—for example, a bell, a spoon in a bowl, the rustling of paper, water being poured from a jug.

✓ Creative play in the kitchen, or with a dolls' house, will allow him to talk about what he is doing.

✓ Repeat the words several times to him.

✓ Explain to him what words mean.

✓ Accept approximations if he doesn't choose the correct word—don't correct him all the time.

✓ Break the word or sentence down into syllables.

✓ Look for books that allow the child to join in and finish off sentences—repetition gives him the feeling of familiarity.

✓ Try 'blowing' games to help with oral motor control —blowing balloons, bubble-blowing, using kazoos, or straw painting.

3 Play—What Can You Do?

Helping the child who has developmental co-ordination disorder (DCD) and dyspraxia should be a pleasure for both child and parent and should not be looked on as a task that *has* to be done.

Play should be:

- Enjoyable
- Help motor co-ordination
- Increase social skills
- Help with getting better language skills

The child with dyspraxia will have problems with:

- How to play
- When to play
- Where to play
- What to play with
- Who to play with

STAGES OF PLAY

- Alone
- Alongside
- With another one-to-one
- With a group

Play that is enjoyable will be something the child wants to be repeated, and this positive experience is a good basis to learn from. The child with co-ordination problems may have difficulty knowing *how* to play games. He will need you to play with him and help him through the process. First of all, try to talk to him at any opportunity. Sometimes, when a child doesn't talk to you, there seem to be fewer chances to talk to him. Whenever you can, ask him what to do next and why. For example, ask him, 'What shall we make with this piece of card?' or 'What shall we pretend this box is?'

This two-way conversation enhances the child's ability to describe a situation and encourages the use of link words like 'on', 'in', 'over', 'through'—all words that he needs to practise. He cannot be expected to do this by himself. You will need to be prepared to give him time. Playing with your child's peers may be difficult for him, especially when the friend takes over or gets cross because yours doesn't know what to do. You may need to supervise to keep him on task and encourage him. Handle the situation sensitively—his confidence to try new things may already be poor. He needs to be praised when he has succeeded. At the same time he will know when he is being patronised.

Always help your child to feel success. Where this is maintained, he will be more inclined to carry on.

Functions of play

- Play allows the child to develop new skills through observation, exploration, discovery and imitation.
- It is a pleasurable activity that relieves boredom and frustration.
- It allows a physical release of energy.
- The child is able to learn about people's roles and skills through make-believe and role-play.

THE RULES OF PLAY

The child who has DCD often has problems with understanding the rules of the game and what it means to win and lose. He may be overenthusiastic when winning and distraught when he has lost. These are skills that need to be taught. The child needs to be supported when he starts to play games, otherwise there may be times when he behaves inappropriately and will lose friends. Try to discuss this with him before the event and arrange a signal (for example, placing your hand on his shoulder) if he is going 'over-board'. He can then take 'time out' for a few minutes to compose himself.

Tips to help

✓   Help the child to understand how the game should be played—it may be necessary to repeat the instructions as you go along.

✓   Offer to play in pairs as a way of supporting the child when playing a new game.
✓   Encourage the child to say out loud what he is doing while carrying out the activity.
✓   Give him time to respond.
✓   Talk to the child about winning and losing and the need for an end to the game. Discuss how long the game will last.
✓   Some games need clear boundaries for start and finish. He needs to be told this before you start. Perhaps you could try to get him to repeat them back to you to make sure he has understood.
✓   Allow the child to choose the games he wants to play, intro-ducing new games only when he feels sufficiently confident.
✓   Talk to the child about turn-taking and reassure and praise when he has done this appropriately.

TYPES OF PLAY

- *Creative*—use of language
- *Exploratory*—helps with body awareness
- *Physical*—improves on gross and fine motor function
- *Constructive*—helps with sequencing, language and fine motor function
- *Imaginative*—develops language and can work on all areas

Creative play

This allows the child to use his imagination and allows you as a parent to have an opportunity to get your child to describe what he is doing and also to follow a sequence of activities.

Example: 'Place the hat *on* your head, now put your gloves *in* your pocket, your scarf goes *round* your neck.' Quite often the child will have difficulty with these little words, and he may think quite literally. This allows him to be more imaginative.

✓ *Play shop* by getting tins out of the cupboard. Save empty cartons and boxes. Make money by using buttons or counters, or cut up squares for notes.

✓ *Play 'house'* by using everyday objects—saucepans, wooden spoons, plastic storage containers, dustpan and brush.

✓ *Encourage dressing up* in old clothes, hats, shoes, gloves and sunglasses. Have a box with these items so that your child can choose to do these activities when he wants to or when he feels like it.

✓ *Garages*. Use toy cars, shoeboxes, children's tools and household furniture. Make a road using a large roll of lining paper and encourage your child to colour it in.

✓ *Puppets*. Make them out of old socks, cut them out of card and join together with tacks, try shadow puppets, model face masks out of papier-mâché. Your child may find it easier to talk to you 'through' the puppet when he is having problems.

✓ *Dolls and doll's houses*. Make rooms out of shoeboxes or other cardboard boxes, or you can buy commercially available doll's houses.

✓ *Make a Wendy house* out of a blanket or sheet draped over the clothes-horse, or put it over the backs of chairs. Your child can climb in and out and over the chairs.

✓ *Tea parties with dolls and teddies*. You can talk to your child about 'order'—'Give the tea to teddy first and to dolly *second*' and so on.

✓ *Farms*, using toy animals. Make a yard using a large piece of board, blue paper for the duck pond, green paper for fields, and so on. Get the child to move around on all fours with the animals and tractors—this helps his shoulder and hip strength at the same time.

✓ *Cooking*. Use dry substances to weigh and pour. Use your imagination with some objects and pretend they are something else—for example, ping-pong balls for fried eggs, tennis balls for potatoes, polystyrene bits for chips, and so on.

Exploratory play

All these types of play will help the child with motor co-ordination difficulties. Most children have an innate curiosity about themselves and their world. They discover that objects and people exist apart from themselves. Exploration provides the means to find out about the properties and qualities of these other entities. It requires a combination of motor, perceptual and cognitive skills. Motor skills involve muscle movement, perceptual skills enable them to place themselves in the context of the world around them, either visually or auditorily (using eyes and ears), and cognitive skills give them the understanding required. The dyspraxic child may have poor body awareness and not realise where his body is in space in relation to other objects.

Guessing shapes and improving body awareness

✓   Make a 'feely' bag with different items in it. Let the child
    feel them, but not see them, and decide what they are. You
    could choose objects all of the same type—for example,
    different wooden letters or numbers, or pieces of fruit.

✓   They could all be objects of the same consistency—solid or
    soft, wetter as in jelly, spaghetti or baked beans. They could
    be all different consistencies and the child just has to guess
    the texture—whether they are soft, rough, feathery—rather
    than what the object actually is.

✓   Alternatively the child could be blind-folded.

Remember that some children will not like wetter, softer objects
at all and may prefer you to begin with more solid materials.
When you start it may be better to use toys and other familiar
objects for your child to feel before moving on to the wetter,
softer material.

✓   Get the child to follow patterns of movement while lying and
    sitting on the floor—you move and then let him copy you.

Physical play

This is play that involves the development and refinement of
gross motor skills—the large movements of the body such as
those required for running and balancing. It requires the ability to
initiate (start), co-ordinate (put together) and patterning of movements (follow a pattern or sequence).

✓   With the younger child, *rough play* is ideal for the above. It
    is best done with a parent in that the child can follow the
    parent crawling, rolling and climbing over and under the
    furniture.

✓   Play wheelbarrow races and races on knees and/or all fours.
    Start like a commando on your tummy and then on knees
    and then progress to all fours.

✓   Let the child swim on his front and back in a pool, using a
    board to hold on to if necessary. Running through the water
    and getting in and out of the pool will all help, too.

✓   A climbing frame lets him get his feet off the ground, but be
    there to support him. You may need to hold him while he
    climbs to begin with.

Constructive play

This involves the integration of motor and sensory skills in an activity, which results in an end product—for example, building a tower with blocks. It also requires the intellectual processes of memory, storage and retrieval. The child needs to be able to follow a pattern and remember from previous experience how it was done.

✓   Lego Duplo, which has big pieces, is a good starting point. You could part construct and let the child fill in gaps, or use it to colour-match a row of red pieces, then one of green. From this you could move on to practise sequences with your child. Place two yellow bricks followed by three red, and then two more yellow, and get the child to copy the pattern.

Imaginative play

Fundamental to this type of play is the use of objects or gestures to represent other objects or events that are not present. It is characterised by make-believe and role-play activities. Imitation, motor, sensory and cognitive skills are central to its development. It helps the use of language at all levels.

✓   Give your child an empty cardboard box, some coloured pens, paper and glue and let him build anything—a TV, a boat, a post office. Let him talk to you about what he is doing.
✓   Let him have some 'dressing-up' clothes and some empty food boxes and let him play school or shops.
✓   Put together a puppet show.
✓   Play travel agents or post office.

The child with DCD may like to play 'younger' style games rather than those for his age group and should be allowed to do so. He may be showing you that he is not ready to move on, and does not have the language and motor skills required for more complex play.

*   *   *

The child with dyspraxia or developmental co-ordination disorder (DCD) may have a variety of problems that need addressing.

Home is often a safe environment to learn how to play games and join in, without the fear of competition and criticism. He may have had experiences in school which make him reluctant even to try to join in with a new game. The level you may need to play with your child might seem very simple for his age group, but if he is enjoying it and concentrating on playing, this is a result in itself. You may find that at the end of a school day your child is very tired. Trying to 'play' with him then could just be too much. It may be better to do this at the weekend or in the holidays when he is more relaxed and receptive.

Games can be played indoors and outdoors or anywhere the child likes. Let him be involved in planning a game and take a lead from him. He should be able to understand the object of the game and to participate fully for it to be of value. It is sometimes better to start off with what appears to be a very simple game, which gives him a feeling of success. This is preferable to trying a game which is claimed to be for his age group but is in fact too hard for that particular child at this time.

At this age the child will often have already realised that he is not as good as others with ball games, PE activities, climbing or riding his bike. He will watch other children in the playground and want to join in. He will also want to gain the skills that allow him to do so.

Continued failure, and being apart from his peers in games and play, serve to strengthen his feelings of inadequacy. He may gradually become more isolated and withdrawn. It is possible that he may refuse to join in and may even use his problems as an excuse. More and more he expects to fail instead of feeling he might succeed. As a consequence of this, his peers may see him as stubborn and unwilling to try. They may misinterpret his past (bad) experience as 'bad behaviour', whereas in fact it is usually that he does not want to set himself up to fail yet again.

GAMES TO IMPROVE GROSS AND FINE MOTOR SKILLS

Always think big first. Improving gross motor skills—concentrating on working on hips and shoulder strength—will have a knock-on effect on fine motor function and the smaller movements. The games described will often work on both areas at the same time, as well as helping language skills and number work.

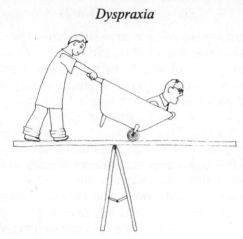

Games to help gross motor skills

✓ *Create an assault course.* For example, crawl under and over duvets and pillows, behind chairs and under a coffee table. Turn the game into an adventure story by collecting treasure *en route*. Encourage your child to use his imagination, and let him build his own course by planning which component comes next. Have a surprise at the end of it—a book to read to him, or give him a drink.

✓ *Ball games.* Use larger balls, or slow-moving items such as balloons or scarves to catch or hit. Roll balls to one another while sitting on the floor. If your child's catching is poor, roll a ball off the edge of the table and encourage him to catch it—even get him to hold a basket to catch it with. Play lots of target games, knocking items over or through narrowing goal posts.

✓ *Bat and ball games.* There are some very nice 'big bats' available from toyshops. Use them to hit 'koosh' balls, balloons, or large shuttlecocks. If you start by using large items, the child will see success before you move to a smaller bat with a smaller surface area.

Large golf clubs and balls, shuttlecocks for badminton, spongy bats and balls are all easily available. The DCD child often has difficulty co-ordinating his eyes and hands. These larger and slower-moving objects make it easier to work on this and therefore success is more likely to be achieved. 'Scatch', a catching game where the ball suckers onto a Velcro pad, is a fun way to promote eye/hand co-ordination. If the 'paddles' are on both hands, then left and right discrimination can also be improved.

✓ *Trampolines and bouncy castles* are great to help encourage balance and posture. The child can also relate to other children and it promotes turn-taking.

✓ *Creative activities like painting.* Use 'tools' with large chunky handles. Try different ideas like DIY paintbrushes, easy paints in pots, large chalks or painting crayons. Often the child with co-ordination difficulties dislikes pencil tasks, and you will therefore need to be innovative in choosing different tools and techniques to encourage him. It may be easier for the child to work vertically rather than on a table. Try putting up paper on a wall or paint a blackboard area—it will help your child's shoulder strength. Painting could be done in the kneeling position to help improve hip stability.

✓ *Make collages and constructions* using 'rubbish'—for example, make a robot out of cornflakes boxes and toilet roll holders. Let the child use his imagination. He may not have as much time in school because of the extra time it takes him to complete a task.

✓ *Tearing and scrunching paper* is really good for hand strength. Crêpe paper and newspaper tear easily, but card is easier to hold.

✓ *Clay, soft stuff, bread dough, salt dough* are also useful to promote hand and shoulder strength. Try burying coins inside a ball of clay and ask your child to find them. This makes the fingers work really hard. The harder the plasticine or clay, the more the child has to work. If you put this in the fridge before playing with it, it will make it even harder!

✓ *Construction activities* are essential for the child with poor motor co-ordination. He will often find it hard to pull things apart and push them together again. If he gets frustrated with Lego, try something less resistive like Stickle Bricks or magnetic blocks. Popoids are another construction toy that the child can try, or let him put together something like a marble maze or the game 'Mouse Trap', both of which have a game at the end of the construction. Get him to do this on all fours as well as in a sitting or a high kneeling position.

✓ *Target games.* These types of game promote the ability to judge distances and therefore the ability to gauge how much force is required to throw an object. Often the child has difficulty with this and consistently misjudges how forceful to be. This skill also includes the ability to know when to let go. Practise rolling games first at larger targets, such as *skittles*. Try using quoits or *boule* sets, or *darts* using a Velcro board. A dartboard can be good for eye-hand co-ordination; there are Velcro ones available that are safe.

✓ *French skipping-ropes*. These are good for gross motor co-ordination, taking turns, rhythm and sequencing. You can recite or sing rhymes.

TRADITIONAL GAMES
✓ Tag, British Bulldog, Red Rover, Tug o'War, On the Way to London, Hopscotch are all great for turn-taking and for listening skills. Some demand good co-ordination, so do be mindful of this. You may need to adapt the game slightly in order for your child to complete it successfully.

RACES
✓ *Wheelbarrow races*. Ensure you provide good support under the child's thighs, and mind your own back. This activity is great for the muscles around the shoulders and the arms.
✓ *'All fours races'*. Race on all fours up and down a room in the house in order to collect tokens. Get him to play with his peers or siblings. Commando crawling (on his tummy) is very good for strength and co-ordination of his limbs.
✓ *Log rolling* (body in a straight line). This is good for the trunk.
✓ Use large cardboard boxes (take the staples out) and get him to roll in these or to crawl on all fours to make it move forwards. Manoeuvre over pillows or cushions. Roll and knock over skittles.

Games to help fine motor skills

GAMES YOU CAN BUY IN THE SHOPS
✓ Lego, Duplo, Stickle Bricks, Popoids, Art Straws, Tap o'Shape, Meccano.
✓ Use threading activities—Hungry Hippos, PegBoards, Pick-up sticks.

These are a few of the games available commercially which help with dexterity.

If your child has difficulty manipulating objects, use brick blocks, buttons, Duplo and so on, as they are easier to hold and move.

If pull and push apart is hard, try initially using games which offer less resistance, like magnetic bricks or Stickle Bricks. Not only do these activities promote dexterity, they also promote hand strength and co-ordinated use of right and left hands, eye/hand co-ordination and a variety of perceptual and language skills (see Glossary for terms used).

OTHER GAMES YOU CAN PLAY

✓ *Pastry and bread dough making* are good for promoting fine motor skills and tolerance to different textures.

✓ *Use clothes pegs* to hang dolls' clothes on a small line or clip them around a shoebox. Use a dice and encourage your child to take the correct number of pegs out of the box—that is, to correspond with the dots on the dice. Look out for different-sized pegs to promote more dexterity or strength.

✓ *Make hedgehogs* using Play-doh. Use halves of cocktail sticks or used matches (take ends off) to make the spines.

✓ *Post money* into a money-box.

✓ *Post marbles* into plastic lemonade containers.

✓ *Sequencing and pattern matching-*. The child may find copying from a diagram difficult. Help him by making a simple design which he has to copy, and then increase the complexity of the task.

✓ *Use large, simple puzzles*, but choose ones that appeal to your child and do not offend him as being too babyish. Peg games with a pegboard allow him to copy a shape, see patterns and colour-matching as well. They also help with sequencing skills and language concepts.

✓ *Computer games*. Look for those that use a mouse for eye/hand co-ordination. Games which require the child to follow instructions, or which have a problem-solving element in them, are also useful. There is a larger 'mouse' available that is easier to manipulate. Keyboards based on ABC rather than QWERTY could be considered.

ACTIVITIES FOR CHILDREN OVER ELEVEN YEARS OLD
(See also chapter 9)

Younger children with co-ordination problems will often be more willing to join in activities with their family. In the case of an older child, however, his experiences in school and his lower self-esteem may mean that he does not want to bother to start to play a game of cards or a board game. He may have become more socially isolated and be more reluctant to participate in anything.

Often the child may appear to be less mature than his peers. If allowed, he will choose games that a younger child likes, but he will also be aware that he wouldn't want to do this in front of his peer group. He may still need to improve many of the necessary foundation skills. If he has a younger brother or sister, let him join in with some of their activities: it will be more acceptable to play with them.

Tips to help

✓ It may still be just as much fun at eleven or twelve to play catch as it was at five.

✓ Make a target to throw the ball into—a netball or basketball net, not set too high. In the house you could use bean-bags and a waste-paper bin.

✓ Mini-golf or football between the two of you does not have to be competitive.

✓ Allow him to help you in the kitchen. Cooking is very good because of the stirring, mixing, rolling and cutting—all useful tasks. Clearing up, washing and drying and wiping surfaces can also be helpful.

✓ Cleaning windows with both hands can be enjoyable and will help with co-ordination—therapy does not have to be obvious to the child. Laying the table (understanding right and left and having to pattern-match) is also helpful—you could lay one place and then get your child to do the rest.

Any construction activities will help

✓ Meccano is something your child can do at his own pace.

✓ Also available are kits to make plantpot holders and birdhouses—why not let him try some of these? A visit to your local craft shop may be worthwhile.

✓ Making a simple balsawood plane with help from a parent can be enjoyable. Let your child take the lead in what he chooses to do. Do not try to 'play' for too long—he or she will get tired and frustrated and will be reluctant to do the activity again.

✓ The child often resists therapy at this age, and help should not be too obvious to him. It is better that the tasks relate to the activities of daily living, and aim to increase the functionality for the child.

✓ Taking turns and understanding the rules of the game will still be difficult concepts for many adolescents to learn. Start with simple card games and move on to other games such as Monopoly. It will help him with counting and sequencing difficulties as well. If he is wary, let him 'help' you to start. He could act as the banker in Monopoly, or partner you in a game. Some traditional games are now made for the computer, such as Scrabble and Yahtzee, and this allows the child to learn the rules and practise his skills before playing with others. However, it is a good idea for him to play with others as well, in order to practise his social skills.

4 Everyday Skills for the Child

The child with dyspraxia may have problems in several areas in which other children learn to manage once they have gone to nursery or on to school. At the nursery stage in their development however, many children are still not accomplished at completing these tasks and still require adult support and supervision. The areas of difficulty may include eating and drinking, dressing and undressing, managing the toilet and cleaning themselves afterwards.

EATING AND MEALTIMES

Mealtimes can be a disaster zone for these children, When a child eats a meal he has to be able to accomplish several tasks at once. The first of these is to sit on a chair and remain in one position and not fall off. Once he has accomplished this and is stable, he needs to be able to use cutlery and negotiate drinking from a cup.

At the pre-nursery stage the child may use a high chair which provides him with a footrest for balance and a tray in front of him on which to eat his food. The tray is positioned at hip height and at the correct distance from him. Parents then often transfer the child to a booster seat, or just let him sit on a kitchen chair. If this is done, his legs may dangle down and not rest on the floor for support. An additional problem is that the table tends to be at his chest level rather than at hip height. To increase his difficulties, we go from giving him children's utensils to using adult-size cutlery, which is often far too big for a child's hands. The grip on the handle may be slippery and the angle may make it harder to cut or hold his food. What was a simple act of sitting at the table is now stressful and difficult to do well. He may well feel like he is sitting at the 'giant's table'.

The child is then made to sit and eat and attend to his food three times every day. Without carefully looking at the table, the chair, cutlery and cup to see if these are correct for the child, we are not giving him a chance to acquire the skills of cutting up his food and being able to drink from a cup.

If you observe a young child with co-ordination difficulties trying to pour from a jug or carton into a cup, he may spill a great deal of the drink. He may try to hold the carton close to his body to improve the stability that he requires to complete the task. A full cup may also be difficult, as his movements may not be good enough to be able to drink slowly, and he may end up spilling it. The child may require a feeder cup with a lid for longer than other children, or may need to have his cup not overfilled.

✓ Make sure the child is sitting with his feet firmly on the floor and that the table is at hip height.
✓ Use appropriately sized cutlery. Try bending 'cheap' cutlery at an angle to help with eating. Use a piece of foam tubing to help with the grip. Buy some cutlery which is made specifically for the child—for example, Caring Cutlery or Maws.
✓ Use a piece of Dycem or a facecloth that has been wrung out and place this under the plate to stop it moving around.
✓ Use a soup bowl or plastic bowl with a lip, to limit the spread of the food. The child can scoop more easily.
✓ Do not overfill the cup or plate. The child can always have more.
✓ Play some games to help with eating skills. The Chocolate

Game requires a dice, a bar of chocolate and clothes to put on and off, such as hat, gloves and scarf. The first person throws the dice, and when he has thrown a six he then starts to put on all the items of clothing and to cut a square of chocolate and eat it. The next person then tries to throw a six. As soon as she has done this the first person has to stop eating and hand everything over, then he starts throwing the dice again, and so on ... This game helps with dressing skills, cutting, and attention and social skills, and could be done in a group of two or three children together. They see the clear reward—to cut and eat as much chocolate as they can until the next six is thrown.

DRESSING AND UNDRESSING

Many children at the pre-school stage are still unable to fully dress and undress themselves. They may need extra help with some tasks, like doing up the top button on a coat. The child with co-ordination difficulties will show several problems when dressing. He may need help to get out of his clothes and with the order in which he puts them on. The sequence of dressing needs to be taught as well as the skills of putting on each item. Visual clues may need to be given. You may need to guide the child in what to put on next and which way round it goes.

✓ If you are in a rush, help the child with most of the dressing and leave just the clothes that he can do for himself.

✓ Teach dressing skills when you are both not in a rush.

Buttoning and unbuttoning

Because of the fine motor difficulties the child will find this a problem. This is especially true when he cannot see the buttons, especially the one at the top of a shirt.

✓ Use a dressing doll to practise on.

✓ Practise threading beads.

Zips

Doing up zips may be difficult, especially if the child is unable to see what he is doing. He may not be able to grasp hold of the small zip puller, or to slot a zip into its holder in a jacket and then pull it up.

✓ You can attach a zip puller or a toggle on the end, or use a metal loop, like a key ring, to make it easier.

✓ Practise with clothes off the child—on a hanger or dressing doll or on the floor—before practising on the child himself.

The child may find he cannot work out which way he should put his clothing on, and end up putting things on back to front. When putting something over his head he becomes disorientated and does not know where his body is in space.

Shoes

Putting shoes on the correct feet may be difficult. The child cannot see and does not understand how to follow his feet into the shoe, so the act of getting the shoe on at all may be a problem, as well as doing it up.

✓ Velcro makes this very easy.

✓ Learning to tie a bow may be much harder for him, as he may not be able to see where to place one lace over or under the other one, or have the manual dexterity to hold one bit while moving another lace.

✓ Use different-coloured laces joined together so that he can see which is which when you are teaching him: 'Put the *black* lace over the *white* lace.'

✓ Use a practice shoe first before trying this on his foot.

Gloves

Putting on finger gloves may be a difficult task to accomplish. The DCD child may not have good awareness of where his fingers are once he has placed them inside the glove. It is often easier for him to use mittens at this stage.

✓ Practise using finger puppets, and getting the child to play with Play-doh which he can poke and prod with his fingers.

Other tips to help

✓ Place pictures of the child's clothes on his drawers—he could help you draw these or colour them in. Think about cutting pictures from magazines to stick on the drawers. Let the child be involved in this as it will help him to remember. He could choose the pictures, help to cut them out and then stick them on to card.

✓ Place the child's clothes in the drawers in the order he will be putting them on—pants at the top, vests next and so on.

✓ Use a 'dressing doll' to help set out his clothes for the next day, or lay them out on the floor or on a hanger where he can see them.

✓ Use Velcro on his shoes, or elastic laces that can be done up and look like ordinary laces, but mean the child can just slip his foot in.

✓ Try Bungy laces. These are curly laces that just need to be twisted to do them up and come in a variety of colours.

✓ Put poppers or Velcro on his shirts to make it easier to get dressed and undressed.

✓ Label the clothes with clear tags—it may be easier to use a colour that he can clearly see rather than his name. For example, when there is a large number of coats in a cloak-room, looking for the name is just too hard, but a clear red tag is much easier to identify.

✓ Let him wear jumpers that have an obvious front and back—a V-neck or a sweatshirt with a logo on it will help him to see this more easily.

✓ Place his coat at the end of a row. This will make it easier for him to find it at the end of nursery or in a busy cloakroom at school.

✓   If he needs a shoebag, make it brightly coloured so that he can quickly recognise it.

TOILETING

Passing urine

The child who is low toned may find that when he needs to go to the toilet he wants to go NOW and will not be able to hold on for a long time. Parents will recognise this, when they go on a car journey and need to stop by the side of the motorway several times because their child cannot hang on even five minutes more until the next turn-off! He may have some accidents when he starts at nursery school. This may be because he cannot find the toilet as easily or that he cannot get undressed quickly enough to reach the toilet. The toilet in some places may also be too high for him. Washing and drying his hands may be difficult and he may end up soaked every time he goes to relieve himself.

✓   Make sure he has been shown several times where the toilet is when he first starts at nursery.
✓   He may need a step to help him up.
✓   Elastic trousers or track pants are the easiest clothes to cope with.
✓   Give the teacher a spare set of clothes just in case. Your child will be less embarrassed if he changes into his own clothes rather than the 'spare' pair kept for accidents.

Bowels

The problems can be due to:

- Poor body awareness
- Poor stability
- Less sensation to go to the toilet
- Constipation
- Sequencing problems

Gaining good bowel control is something most children acquire by the age of three. Up to this stage your child will have had a parent to respond to his needs rather than having to think about them himself. Once he goes to nursery school he has to be more independent. If he needs to open his bowels at school he also needs to learn to wipe his bottom.

Children with DCD have a number of problems that can make this whole area difficult for them. First, the child is not always aware of where his body is relative to everything else, so knowing where his bottom is may be hard for him. The second problem may be gaining stability on the toilet. He may be placed with his feet dangling down, so that he cannot apply pressure when opening his bowels. He may even feel as if he is going to fall down the hole in the toilet. He may also forget the sequence of events that will make it a successful task. He may arrive at the toilet knowing why he is there, do what he should do and then get off, forgetting completely about wiping himself clean. These children are usually the ones who are having other sequencing problems.

If he is also low toned, he may not have such clear sensations about when he needs to go and may also become *constipated*. This may become such a problem for him that he has 'overflow' which presents as diarrhoea. He may well be treated for this, which can make the whole problem even worse. He may start to become tearful before going to nursery because of the fear of what might happen while he is there, especially if he has had previous accidents.

Tips to help

✓　Make sure the child is both comfortable and stable on the toilet. Provide him with a step or footrest and even rails to hold on to at the sides of the toilet.

✓　Try not to rush him.

✓ Consider at this age using an inner toilet seat to make sure the hole in the toilet seat is not too big for him.

✓ Put a sign up in your toilet at home to remind the child to wipe his bottom or to ask for help. Even use a sequence of cards showing a seat, toilet paper, flush and taps, to remind him of the whole process.

✓ Try some games passing things through legs and around, with a quoit, for example. You could do this as a team game in school, with an object passing 'over' and 'under' and 'through' legs—use this language as well to work on language skills at the same time. No one needs to know you are practising toilet skills with the class!

✓ Use wet wipes—these have a greater surface area than tissues and are easier to hold. They allow the child to clean himself more easily and have a pleasant smell if he hasn't done the job perfectly!

✓ Establish a regular time for him to go to the toilet. At home encourage him to go after breakfast, and make sure that he is given enough time. This takes advantage of something known as the 'gastro-colic reflex' and gets his bowels used to being opened regularly. The child then knows to go to the toilet before going to school.

✓ Make sure his diet encourages good bowel movement—a bran-based cereal or a banana or other fruit cut up on top of the cereal will help.

✓ Make sure the child is drinking enough—he may be reluctant to drink because he will need to urinate more. He may be offered less to drink because he spills it. This will also make it more likely that he will become constipated.

✓ Check with him when he comes home from school that he has been to the toilet. He may have avoided it all morning because of fear of an accident.

✓ Encourage him to tell you if he has had an accident and offer him help rather than telling him off. He may even resort to hiding his pants from you if he sees that he will get into trouble.

FATIGUE

Children with co-ordination problems often seem to get more tired than others in their peer group. The child has to concentrate more to complete any task. He will often be better performing earlier in the day rather than later. He may not be able to do some things in the afternoon that he could do in the morning. When he comes home from nursery at the pre-school stage he may still require a sleep in the afternoon to recover from the morning's activities. He may not concentrate as well after a period of intense concentration and may require some recovery time. If you can choose which time he goes to nursery, consider morning sessions first, when he will be at his most alert.

SLEEP DISTURBANCE

The child with dyspraxia may always have been a restless sleeper.

✓   Give him time to calm down before bed.
✓   Increase his physical activity in the late afternoon so that he is physically tired.
✓   Establish a routine—bath, story and bed.
✓   A massage with a carrier oil (this can be a sunflower oil) with some lavender oil drops in it may help to relax the child before bed. Massage firmly. He may find light touch feels painful and does not give him enough feedback.
✓   Is the bedroom too light or dark, too cold or too warm?
✓   He may feel more comfortable with greater weight on him rather than a duvet—consider using blankets and tucking him in. He will feel more secure and it will give his body the messages that he needs to settle him down. A wedge of pillows may also help.
✓   Place his bed against the wall to increase his sense of security.
✓   Try using a sleeping-bag.

5   The Child in School

The child with co-ordination difficulties needs to be understood by his teacher. A sensitive approach will allow him to get the best out of each day, and the teacher to get the best out of the child. It is worth remembering a few key elements to make this an all-round success. The teacher may well be trying to cope with a big mixed ability class, and at the same time be trying to give time to the children with specific difficulties. This is a balancing act. It is far better to tailor all activities to the whole class so that they can all benefit. The ideas suggested can be used for *all* children and not just those with specific problem areas.

✓   Watch the child in the playground—he may be the target of bullies.

✓   Easy tasks given to other children may be difficult for this child—dinner time, for example, when trying to pour a drink or pass a plate to someone else.

Reading and writing

✓   Don't expect the pupil to redraft written work. He will usually have tried his hardest the first time.

✓   Don't make the child read aloud if he is uncomfortable.

✓   Consider whether he is happy with the appearance of his work before putting it on the wall. It may be necessary to retype it for him.

✓   Allow extra time to complete a task, and do not punish him when work has not been completed. It is not helpful to get him to complete the work in playtime or after school, as this suggests to him that he is being punished because of his problems, despite trying his hardest. He will also get tired more easily.

✓   Place the child near the front where he can have good eye contact with you and the board, but place him away from the main thoroughfare of traffic where he may be knocked, and from the window where he may be distracted more easily.

✓   Make sure that his desk and chair are at the right height —feet on the floor and the desk at hip height.

✓   Any instructions need to be given in small, bite-size pieces. If necessary ask him to repeat them back to you. Where there are organisational problems you may need to devise timetables, so use colour-coding and picture cues to help the child structure his activities.

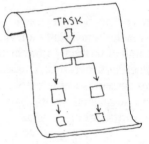

How does the child feel?

✓   Try to understand how hard the child is trying.

✓   Allow 'time out' if the child is obviously tired or unable to concentrate. At times he just won't be able to take in any more information.

✓   Reward him for trying, rather than rewarding him only when he has done well. He will already be failing at other tasks and the thought of trying again and failing, even with a reward at the end of it, may not be a great enough incentive. You may need to take a task back two or three stages if he continually fails. Often, these children have not fully established the foundation skills and ultimately he may need to develop splinter skills just to complete a specific task. Often he may not master the task at all.

✓   Try not to compare him to other class members.

✓ Publicly praise his efforts.
✓ Encourage group working to help with his social interaction.
✓ Allow him to be class monitor to give him some status.

Tools to learn and how to sit

✓ Encourage the use of a pencil case that is 'see-through' so that its contents can be checked. Write out a list of contents to be stapled inside, so that everything can be checked in at the end of the day and after each class.
✓ Use a clipboard to hold the paper on which he is working. Place some 'Dycem' on the paper to stop it from slipping.
✓ Pencils with triangular grips may help, but fatter-barrelled or triangular pencils can also help. Give him a selection from which to choose. If there is 'the school pen', consider that greater choice may be necessary for this child. We don't all wear the same size shoes!
✓ If using a ruler is difficult, place a thin piece of Blu-tack at each end to hold it in place when drawing lines. Rulers with the little handles or roller rulers are also helpful.
✓ A sloping board to work on may make handwriting easier.
✓ He may need a wedge on his seat to position him properly with his feet on the floor.
✓ Place an upturned file on the desk to act as a temporary sloping surface for the child.
✓ Place a telephone directory under his feet if they are dangling down and do not touch the floor.
✓ In the science room, consider that the child may be better standing rather than feeling unsafe perched on a bar stool.

Recording his work

✓ Use different colours on the board to indicate different areas of work.
✓ Repeat new information.
✓ Allow use of a tape-recorder, calculator or laptop. Photocopy sheets for him to fill in answers, rather than having to write out whole passages of work.
✓ Make sure that any homework is written down for the child and that the correct books are in his bag.
✓ Encourage a friend in the class to act as a 'buddy' to help

him around the school, and allow the buddy to remind him
of the work being done.

Communication and social skills

✓   When giving any commands, ensure that there is good eye
contact between you.

✓   Encourage the child to share his possessions, even when
there may be some reluctance.

✓   Give him time out from the other children. If he is getting
overexcited he may need to come in five minutes early from
break time to give him a chance to settle back to work.

✓   Be consistent—the more guidance the child has, the easier
it is for him to cope.

✓   Encourage him to seek out information in areas that he
already appears to be interested in. It will allow him to be an
expert and raise his standing with his peer group. He may
decide on an area that is very different from those of his
classmates.

✓   Accept that fidgety and clumsy behaviour is not always his
fault.

✓   Use positive terminology with the child—for example,
'enthusiastic', 'alert', 'inquiring'. The child will use this
feedback to himself, and it will raise his or her self-esteem.

Different activities around the school

✓   Allow extra time for the child to change for PE and get back
to the lesson.

✓   Suitable clothing for the child helps. If there is a uniform,
then trousers with elasticised top, ties on elastic and Velcro
shoes all help the child to cope better. It is always better that
he gets to the PE class at the same time as others, rather than
be ten minutes late and never be chosen for the team.

COPING IN PE CLASS AND OTHER PHYSICAL
GAMES IN SCHOOL

✓   Be aware and understand the child's current difficulties.
Previous failure may mean that he will not even try a new
activity, even if it is at a simple level and achievable.

✓ Develop positive attitudes—for example, help to teach the child how to cope with both success and failure and give as much encouragement as possible. Allow him to work against himself and not against others—'you have improved since last week'.

✓ Help him respond readily to simple instructions and signals (don't give too many sequences of instruction at one time). For example: 'Class, quickly line up in six rows of five children, facing the front of the gym, legs astride, hands on heads.' The child may only be able to hold on to the first or the last instruction and be lost, when the other children have already started the activity.

✓ Be aware that the child may use strategies to avoid carrying out tasks he finds difficult. He may become the class clown, or decide he needs to go to the toilet in the middle of the lesson to avoid joining in. However, he may also genuinely need to go.

✓ Position the child where you can ensure that he is not near a window or door, or at the back of the gym, field or pool.

✓ Make sure the child can *hear* the commands clearly if given verbally, or can *see* the game plan if written on a board. Some instructions may need to be repeated by the child, to ensure that he has heard and understood them. You may need to show him the actions you want as well as telling him.

✓ If the child has poor planning abilities, break down the skills, activities or tasks into smaller components.

✓ Ensure that, as far as possible, the child joins in with the sessions without losing confidence and self-esteem. If he is unable to, he should be given activities to assist with the task being taught such as ball skills for eye/hand co-ordination prior to playing a team game like netball or basketball. Ideally, if there are other children of a similar ability, they can all improve their skills by practising together as a group.

✓ Warm-up exercises will help the child to concentrate on the task.

✓ Consider how to help the individual child but fit this into whole class activities—for example, working on pelvic girdle strength, games on their knees, catching and throwing.

✓ Be aware that difficulties may manifest themselves again, especially during sudden growth spurts when bones grow faster than muscles. In puberty, menstruation may also affect ligamentous elasticity around the pelvis and lower back. This may give pain and greater instability, affecting balance and co-ordination.

✓ If the child previously had problems with pelvic girdle instability, his hamstring muscles may have shortened as a means for the trunk to gain stability around the pelvic girdle. This will be apparent in periods of long sitting and during warm-up stretches. It is important not to 'stretch' these muscles in isolation, as the pelvic girdle and lower trunk will become unstable and balance and co-ordination will become affected.

✓ If he is posturally unstable, the child may be unable to sit unsupported, for example in a circle. He may need to sit with his back to a wall.

✓ Avoid team games for which he is likely to be the last to be chosen.

✓ Think about sports day. The dressing game, the egg-and-spoon race and the obstacle race may be even harder for the child with co-ordination problems. Consider a team approach and reward with 'stickers or certificates' for trying, not only for first, second and third positions.

✓ Ask the child to be the umpire or captain. Let him select the team if you have to have one.

Games to help gross motor function

✓ *Twirling*. Using foam or plastic tubing or scarves, or ribbons on sticks, to make patterns in the air. The child could draw out words for other children to guess.

✓ *Parachute*. Using a silk parachute, get the whole class to make waves, then they should run under the parachute all together. They can then swap positions or run around the parachute.

✓ *Water painting*. All the children can paint the outside of the school with water and big paintbrushes—do this in the sitting position, on all fours, kneeling or squatting.

✓ *Commando crawling*. Create an assault course in the gym for the class to crawl around. They could construct this themselves in small teams and then time the teams.

✓ *Balloon and bats or poles*. Move more slowly and give the children a chance of success. The children can work in pairs.

✓ *French skipping*. This is good for rhythm and social skills as well as co-ordination. You could get the children to sing rhymes while they skip.

✓ *Different positions*. Standing, high-kneeling, lying down —any exercise can be done in a variety of positions to work on the different muscle groups.

✓ *Work from big to small*, not from small to big. You want to gain good shoulder control to improve gross motor skills and then fine motor skills.

✓ *Play musical statues*.

Activities in PE to help with handwriting

✓ Running right and left—any directional games where the child has to listen and understand in order to follow instructions will be helpful.

✓ Mark out the floor with a design—this could be a square to start with and become more complicated. Get the children to run along it, crawl, creep, go on knees. Talk about going up, down, to the right and to the left. Let the child tell you where he is going.

✓ Work on the child's back and front to improve body awareness.

✓ Rhythm work—start first of all marching slowly and then faster to different music, first of all just working on legs and then arms as well. This will help with the rhythm of writing and the language required

Activities in PE to help with personal skills

✓ Use quoits in teams—pass under and over to the person behind—for toileting skills.

✓ Use hoops to climb through and pass over the head and down—for dressing.

ACTIVITIES IN THE CLASSROOM TO PROMOTE LISTENING SKILLS

Experiment with objects or musical instruments, emphasising the sounds.

✓ Get the children to join in with rhymes and songs, doing the actions.

✓ Repeat rhymes that the children get to know, then leaving a pause for the class to put in the missing words.

✓ Tell stories—pausing for the child to join in. A good example is 'The Three Little Pigs' . . . huffs and puffs.

✓ Hide a ticking clock and ask him to find it.

✓ Clapping games.

✓ Sound lotto. This is a game with an audiotape with different sounds that need to be matched to a board of different pictures (available from Early Learning Centres and other large toy shops).

✓ Make up a story with the child's name in it. When the child hears his name he must put up his hand.

✓ Following commands. Use 'Simon Says': 'Put one hand on your tummy and one hand on your head'.

✓ Sit children in a circle and when their name is called, they must catch a ball.

✓ Create a rap song with the class. This provides rhythm and poetry. It could be based on something the class is studying currently, or choose a topic they enjoy. They could write the rap, with one child being the shouter and the class responding, working on timing and increasing social interaction. The child could start off with just a repeated question to the class —for example, 'Where do you go?' Response: 'We go to school.' Then: 'What do you do?' Response: 'We do some work.' 'Why do you do it?' Response: 'So we can learn.'

✓ Use a drum and make the words of a familiar poem or song fit the beat. You can increase and then slow the beat. Let the children in the class walk to this and move in time to the music.

HAND EXERCISES TO IMPROVE CO-ORDINATION

All children need time to warm up their hands and fingers in the morning. This is useful for the child who needs to strengthen his hands which still show marked weakness. You will see him gripping tightly on to his pen and his hands may ache after trying to write for some time. These simple exercises could be done at the start of each lesson. Get all the children to do the following:

✓ Grip thumbs around each other into a loop and pull them in the opposite direction.

✓ Place palms together and push hands together as if you were praying.

✓ Place hands under legs while sitting down, and lift yourself up.

✓ Tear strips of paper and then roll up a strip, gathering the strip towards you, first with one hand and then with the other.

✓ Pick up raisins with your finger and thumb. Use both hands simultaneously or alternate hands.

✓ Pass a pencil along your fingers, starting with your thumb. Roll it over and under and back again.

✓ Squeeze a soft ball like a Theraball—these are particularly good as they come in different strengths, which can make it harder or easier to squeeze. You could also use a 'stress' ball.

✓ Use some Play-doh that has been slightly hardened in the fridge. Place a coin in the centre of it and get the child to find the coin.

✓ Rolling, threading and cutting all isolate finger movements and will help strengthen fingers and improve hand function.

OTHER IDEAS

✓ *Games with a yo-yo* need to separate the thumb to work them properly and improve the child's eye/hand function as well as co-ordination.

✓ *Cats' cradle* is an old-fashioned game with elastic or wool, making patterns with this with your fingers.

✓ *French knitting.* Winding around a bobbin to make long 'snakes' that can be turned into coil mats can be both fun and help hand dexterity.

✓ *Squeezy bottles*. Fill bottles with paint and let the child have a large sheet of paper on which he can make big movements, squirting the paint out. A thick or thin consistency of paint could be used to make it harder to squeeze out the paint.

✓ *Paint and sand letter formation*. Mix paint and sand together to give some texture to the writing. Let the child use his fingers and then the end of a pencil, then a brush.

✓ *Tactile letters*. Feel the shapes as well as seeing and saying them.

✓ *Tracking games*. Follow a balloon in the air: use two balloons and broom handles and get two children to pass the balloons back and forth to each other. Create a marble maze and get the child to follow the ball around the course. Play dot-to-dot games, following a pattern.

✓ *Make letters* from clay or Play-doh.

✓ *Drawing letters and shapes on hands*. One child does this and the other guesses. This is difficult for the child with dyspraxia as he may have poor body awareness.

✓ *Let him draw in a sandbox* using a stick, or a large rake. Let him copy shapes. He could do this kneeling, on all fours, lying or walking.

✓ *Tracking on a board*. Paste spots or shapes on to a board and let the child join up the spots to make a shape—large dot-to-dots.

SCISSOR SKILLS

Before deciding what to do you need to establish exactly what skills you need before you even put a pair of scissors in a child's hands.

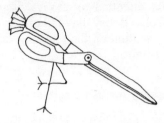

Developmental stages to be passed before using scissors

1 Head and shoulder control

Children develop control of movements in a head-to-toe direction. They learn head control and shoulder control before walking or before fine motor skills are achieved.

A child learns to control the joints closest to his body before being able to control the joints farthest away. He learns to reach and control shoulder movement before achieving elbow, wrist and finger control.

2 Stability before mobility

Infants gain control of their shoulders through the process of lying on their tummy and moving their weight from side to side and forward and backward. Control is further refined as the infant crawls on all fours. As the shoulders gain stability, the weight-bearing and weight-shifting activities in the elbows and wrists stabilise the joints to allow improved fine motor control.

3 'Whole body' movements

4 Separating body movements

Young infants first 'reach' with both arms, with legs, eyes and even with the mouth! Gradually they learn to separate their movements so that one arm, the legs and the mouth can rest quietly as the other arm effectively reaches. In grasping, first the whole hand is used. All fingers do the same thing at the same time.

5 Separating thumb and finger movements

At the next stage the child learns to move his thumb separately and in opposition to the fingers and to use fingers separately for the refined demands of precise gripping.

Children must pay attention to survival issues first. If they are unbalanced and feel as if they may fall off the chair, they will concentrate all their attention on their seating rather than or the fine motor task being taught.

Basic skills necessary for using scissors

- *Balance*. The child must be able to sit in an upright posture, with feet placed firmly on the floor or on a stool or footrest. He must be comfortable and have no fear of tipping over. Attention will then be freed to focus on the task of learning to use scissors.
- *Shoulder stability*. The ability to stabilise and control the movement of the shoulders is important for direct reaching and to provide support for the forearm, wrist and finger actions required in cutting. The child must be able to control both shoulders so that the arms can perform separate actions without losing precision.
- *Forearm control*. The child must be able to move the forearms comfortably from a palm-down (pronated) position to a thumb-up (neutral) position to a palm-up (supinated) position. Not only must he have the range of motion necessary to achieve these movements, but also the movements must be done smoothly and with control.
- *Wrist stability*. The child must be able to hold his wrists in a controlled position and gradually move them into and out of that stable position. When using two hands for cutting, the wrists each move separately in a graded or controlled way. One hand, holding the paper, moves in one direction while the other hand, holding the scissors, moves in a different direction.
- *Grasp*. The ability to close the hand in a cutting motion is required. One hand must hold the paper, using a grasp on the radial (thumb) side of the hand. The other hand must be able to use the thumb, index finger, and middle finger to control the scissors while the other side of the hand is stabilised.
- *Finger isolation*. The ability to isolate the action of the thumb, middle finger, and the index finger allows the child to control the opening and closing of the scissor blades. To isolate each finger into a separate action requires considerable control.

- *Release*. The ability to release an object from the hand is important when grasping the scissors and the paper. It is also part of the action in cutting. First the child 'grasps' to close the hand, and then 'releases' to open the hand. This results in the up-and-down cutting motion of the scissors.
- *Lead-assist two-hand usage*. This is the ability to use both hands together, with one hand stabilising while the other hand leads in the action. It usually requires hand preferences to be at least emerging. Actually, the stabilising (paper-holding) hand must be slightly active as the lead hand moves to perform the cutting actions around corners and angles. This further complicates the task of cutting.
- *Co-ordination of arm, hand, and eye movements*. The ability to co-ordinate the eyes with the finely graded actions of the shoulders, elbows, forearms, wrists and fingers is required before the child can learn to cut.

Tips for scissor skills

✓ Start with firmer paper as it is easier to cut, and later progress to thinner types, which are less resistant and more difficult to control when cutting. You could use card and then move on to sugar paper, ending with tissue paper.

✓ Start with small pieces as they are easier to manipulate, and progress to larger sizes of paper.

✓ Consider the scissors you give the child to use. If he is left-handed, give him left-handed scissors. If he needs spring-assisted scissors, start with these. There are at least four different types of scissors to help every child be able to cut.

Scissor skill activities

✓ Snip small squares of a strip and use for a collage.

✓ Snip longer strips and make into a paper chain.

✓ Make a picture that involves certain small cuts—for example, a paper plate.

✓ Use wool and stick this on card to make a pattern. Have the child cut along the pattern.

✓ If isolating fingers for placement in the loops remains difficult, you may need to consider the use of specialised scissors such as long-loop scissors or spring-assisted scissors.

✓ Cut strips of wool and thread and make a picture wrapping
the wool around nails or pins placed on a board.

ACTIVITIES TO HELP IMPROVE AUDITORY MEMORY SKILLS

✓ *Describe an event or animal*, for example, leaving the child
to give a one-word answer—'It has stripes and four legs and
looks like a horse. It is a . . . ?'
✓ *Families of words.* For example, what family do pear, apple
and banana belong to? Answer: fruit.
✓ *Opposites.* For example, what is the opposite of black?
Answer: white. And of good? Answer: bad.
✓ *Rapping songs.* Let the child make a rap with others in the
class: 'Today is a day for lots of dance', the class then
responds with the same line. Next line: 'We want to sing
along and chant', and so on. These should be rhythmical and
allow the whole class to join in. The child has to listen carefully to be able to echo the response and stay in time.
✓ *Chinese whispers.* Tell the child a short sentence or word,
and pass it around the class and around again.

✓ *Memory games*. Teach the child a short phrase and then get him to recall it at the end of the lesson. At first this could be after five minutes, gradually extending the time he must remember it.

✓ *Clapping rhythms*. Pair up the class and get them to practise a clapping pattern to each other. This could be done with marching, going from slow to fast, and from short to long strides.

✓ *Building up a series of commands*. Go and get your book and then open it at page 3. Add on another command, but check that the child can carry it out. Success breeds success.

✓ *'I went to the market and bought a . . .'.* Go round the class and let each child have a go at remembering the purchases of all the previous children—for example, 'I went to market and bought an apple.' The next person says 'I went to market and bought an apple and a boat' and so on.

✓ *Listening for key words in a story*. Ask the child to count the number of times a word is said in a story—for example, 'every' or 'what'.

✓ *Recall*. Ask the child one or two simple questions after he has listened to a short passage, and gradually build up the length of the passage and the number of questions. Let the child give responses orally.

ACTIVITIES TO HELP VISUAL MEMORY

✓ Show a child two items, for example a toy dog and a toy car. Now hide them and let the child tell which order they were in. Then build this up to three or four items. When this is successful, tell the child the items and then tell him you will move them, show him and then ask him where they are now.

✓ Move on to shapes—squares, circles and triangles. Start with two shapes and gradually increase the complexity, until the child has to recall a series of different shapes.

✓ Get the child to look at a picture in a book for five minutes and then ask him questions about the picture. This could be simple to start with—for example, 'Was there a boy in the picture?' Then move on to, 'Where was the boy in the picture and what was he doing?' and so on.

6 Helping the Distractible Child

To understand what behaviour should be expected, it is worth considering what you would expect from children of different ages. The child with co-ordination problems may often act more like a child with an emotional age about one to two years behind. His attention span may be more in keeping with this than with that of a child of the same age.

NORMAL DEVELOPMENT OF ATTENTION

0–1 years

During this stage a child is very distractible. His attention flits from object to object to person or event to you. Anything new, such as someone walking past, will immediately distract him.

1–2 years

At this stage the child can concentrate on a concrete task of his choice but does not tolerate intervention by an adult, whether verbal or visual. He may therefore appear obstinate or 'wilful'. The child's attention is single-channelled and he has to ignore all extraneous stimuli in order to concentrate upon what he is doing.

2–3 years

Attention at this stage remains single-channelled—in other words, the child cannot attend to auditory and visual stimuli from different sources. He therefore cannot listen to an adult's directions while he is playing but has to shift his whole attention to the speaker and back to the game with an adult's help.

3–4 years

At this stage the child must still alternate his full attention —visual and auditory—between the speaker and the task. However, he now does this spontaneously, without the adult needing to focus his attention.

4–5 years

The child's attention is now two-channelled: he can understand verbal instructions related to the task without interrupting his activity to look at the speaker. Concentration span may still be short but teaching in a group situation is achievable. The child is at nursery school stage where he will work in small groups for short periods of time.

5–6 years

Auditory, visual and manipulatory channels are now fully integrated. Attention is well established and sustained. The child starts school and attends for long enough to sit through a lesson without becoming distractible, if the conditions are correct.

FACTORS AFFECTING ATTENTION

The child with co-ordination problems may be distracted for a variety of reasons:

* Position in the classroom
* Visual distraction
* Auditory distraction
* Posture
* Poor propioception and body awareness
* Lack of motivation
* Task too difficult or too easy

Emotional and behavioural disturbances may produce attention problems.

Environmental distractions can be too strong for the child to attend to the task in hand. Look at the environment you are expecting him to work in. If it is too colourful and too noisy he may need to be put in a quieter and more neutral environment.

The child may be lacking in motivation for many reasons. Previous failure has an effect on future success. The teacher, the subject, and the other children around can all have an effect on the approach of the child.

The task is developmentally too complex or too simple, so that he is either bored or confused. If the task is too hard for him to accomplish, subsequent easier tasks may not be tried and completed. Too easy, and it is not a challenge. The balance is sometimes hard to achieve. The need to grade the activity is essential.

The materials are uninteresting or the task without purpose. Colouring-in endlessly, for example, has no relevance for the child. If this is tied to an end product it has much more purpose. Consider function for the future in deciding which basic skills are important for him to gain now, and which can be adapted.

The child fails to understand the verbal instructions accompanying the task. He may have a language difficulty at a higher level and may not understand the sequence of commands or the complexity, or the context in which it has been placed. The child feels no sense of achievement upon completion of the task. After many failures he may need to see clear rewards at the end if he is to try to complete the task. If there has been indifference to success before, he may see no reason to be successful now.

What can you do to help?

✓ There is a need for consistency, calm, and structure.
✓ Boundaries need to be clear. He needs to know where he is sitting, and who is looking after him. This is so important for the child. Changes in classroom and teachers will cause him anxiety. He needs to know the plan for each day, and that routines will recur, so that, for example, each Monday is the same. This is important to him.
✓ Try to make up a timetable for the holidays as well so that there is structure there too.
✓ When the child first comes in at the start of the day he needs

time to settle down, to allow him to feel in control. This is especially true after a busy time in the playground.

✓ First of all, place the child away from a window and the main stream of child traffic, where he can be more easily distracted.

✓ Make sure that he is in a good line of eye contact so that he can receive visual cues as well as auditory commands.

✓ Break down instructions into small bits, and repeat each stage for the child if necessary.

✓ Help the child to be organised.

✓ Try to sit him next to the quieter children—noise will stimulate him to be noisier.

✓ Praise, praise and praise again—he needs to know that he is being praised for trying, not just for doing well.

✓ Use a timer to show how long a task will take, or set the timer where the task should be completed, before the buzzer goes off.

✓ Always gain good eye contact before giving instructions. Ask the child to repeat them back to you. Don't forget to keep the words you use to a minimum.

✓ Be certain that the child can see an end to the task. When learning new skills it is often hard for him to concentrate whilst the whole thing is being taught. Try to 'backward chain'—that is, starting with the last component and working your way back to the first. Thus the child sees an immediate end result and gets praise.

✓ Reward the child for listening.

✓ Try not to use negatives when correcting. Try 'Now look at your book' instead of 'Don't look over there.'

✓ Be consistent with your expectations and the consequences of breaking rules.

ATTENTION CONTROL AND LISTENING SKILLS

Visual attention provides a child with information about the physical environment and his relationship with it. It tells him about the physical characteristics of objects and people. It helps him to know where he is in space and makes him aware of his relationships to objects in the environment. As the child's ability to conceptualise and think about what he sees expands, so does his visual attention. Three components of visual attention that affect learning are:

Alerting
This is the transition from waking to an attentive and alert state, which is needed for active learning. A balanced state of arousal enables the child to receive visual information.

Selective information
This is the ability to choose relevant information while ignoring the less relevant information. This skill is dependent on the child's ability to attach some meaning to the visual array or to his reason for attending to a particular task. It forms the basis for *visual figure ground perception* and *visual memory* (see Glossary), and is often a problem for the child with specific learning problems, including the dyslexic and dyspraxic child. He cannot filter out the information he needs to learn.

Vigilance
This is the conscious mental effort to concentrate and persist at a visual task. It allows for greater precision in the discrimination of subtle differences among visual stimuli.

Visual attention is improved when the child is appropriately prepared, both physically and mentally. When he has difficulty with any aspect of visual attention, the adult must be concerned with creating an environment that improves the child's attention and the way he performs a task.

Structuring

✓   Decide how long the child is able to attend—be realistic about this.

✓   Create a structure to the session. The child needs to know the beginning and the end. Use a timer to let him know visually.

✓   Involve the child in the planning of the session, so that he may be more motivated to attend and participate. Let him make the timetable: this incorporates other skills, and teaches organisational skills as well.

✓   The child may need to be placed in a quieter and more

'bland' environment for him to start to attend.

✓ Select activities appropriate to his level of function.

✓ Activities should be of interest to the child—if he likes a particular cartoon character, for example, use that. Interest and motivation are what matter most.

✓ Consider the amount of time needed for completion of the activity. Be realistic for that child: he may need time to settle down before he starts.

✓ Use a combination of familiar and novel activities.

Verbalisation and cueing

✓ Be careful about the type and amount of verbalisation used during an activity—sometimes it can be too distracting.

✓ Use simple commands and face the child. Make sure you have his attention *before* giving the command.

✓ Focus on positive behaviour—for example, say 'look at the paper' rather than 'don't look over there'.

✓ Keep verbal instructions brief and simple, drawing attention to one feature at a time.

✓ Non-verbal cues, such as pointing with a finger, can alert the child to salient features of a task.

Tips to help when teaching the child

✓ *Constraints* on the child's behaviour may often be necessary for learning to take place.

✓ *The child must experience success.* The purpose is primarily to teach him to attend to the task, so start with activities that are short, simple and within his ability.

✓   *Materials must be interesting* to the child.
✓   *Rewards* should be an inherent part of the activity or task; above all he should experience the joy of discovery and satisfaction in completing the task. Use a star chart or stickers, for example.
✓   Should rewards like the above be insufficient, try others such as sweets, crisps or *social rewards*—for example, smiles and praise which must be immediate and consistent so that the child learns to associate them with the task.
✓   *Instructions should be modified* to the child's level of development. He may appear less mature than others of the same age, and this should be taken into account although he should not be patronised.
✓   *Materials should be age appropriate*, but the child's interests are the guiding factors; some may prefer toys that are usually associated with a younger age group. Be guided by each child.

✓   *Teaching should proceed in small steps*; gradually extend the duration and complexity of the stimuli the child is expected to attend to and move towards a more normal environment.
✓   *Sit beside him or her and engage in parallel play*. Begin to extend the child's play by demonstration without interfering in what he is doing. He may respond in one of the following ways:
   ●   He may not appear to notice, but begin to imitate your actions.
   ●   He may stop his play and watch you with interest.
   ●   He may destroy your game.
   In any case, contact has occurred and you have caught the child's attention.
✓   When the child can tolerate the adult and begin to imitate,

small modifications to his own play can be made. For example:

- Push the correct puzzle piece in front of him.
- Add another brick to his train or tower.
- Then move towards him, giving simple verbal instruction immediately ahead of your actions.

✓ Present the child with the chosen task activity materials and allow him to decide what to do with them, without help from you.

ESTABLISHING CONTROL AND FOCUS OF ATTENTION

✓ Present the child with the chosen activity materials and allow him a few minutes' exploratory play.

✓ Before giving any verbal instructions, ensure the child is sitting still and not fiddling with the toys.

✓ Call his name, establish eye contact and deliver a short, simple instruction.

✓ The next step is to gain the child's attention while he is actively engaged in the task. Call his name, say 'look', 'listen', but don't give any instruction until you have established eye contact.

✓ Instructions must be related to the task.

✓ Remember that the child may be even more absorbed in these active games and at first you may have to physically still him before you can get his attention.

✓ Gradually decrease the amount you have to do to gain eye contact.

✓ Keep instructions very short to begin with—for example, 'copy me', 'do this'. Accompany with appropriate gestures and hand movements.

Teaching the child to listen and take in what you say without stopping what he is doing

✓ Stand by the child without speaking until he is aware of you, and then give the instruction.

✓ If the child continues to look at you, encourage him to stick at what he is doing with remarks such as 'don't look up, that's very good'. Repeat the instruction if necessary.

✓ Stand by the child occasionally, while commentating on his activity. He cannot look at you without turning his head or looking up.

ACTIVITIES TO PROMOTE THE TRANSFER OF ATTENTION

Transfer to a child's classroom may be affected by:

✓ *Increasing amount of environmental distraction.* The primary school child may be placed in a very stimulating environment.

✓ *The large class and open layout* increases the number of people present in a given situation. Work on gaining attention control can be carried out in a small group after one-to-one has been successful. Initially it may be necessary to increase the help given to the child, as his attention will probably not be as good as in a one-to-one situation. The prompts can then gradually be faded out.

The child should now be able to work alongside another child doing the same activity.

Increase tolerance by:

✓ including him in a small group of children at a similar level of attention;

✓ seating the child in a partitioned area of his own; later remove the partition and have the child with his back to the class;

✓ including him in normal activities and prompting should his attention lapse;

✓ gradually fading out your involvement;

✓ working with parents and the teachers together with the activities the child is expected to get on with by himself in class. These can then be practised on his own at home.

Remember that failure happens when there is:

✓ lack of consistency;

✓ lack of time;

✓ lack of understanding;

✓ poor response to reinforcement—seeing the good behaviour, not just the bad; unrealistic expectations;

✓ holidays and change in the child's life;

✓ lack of rules or rules that change all the time;

✓ confrontation;
✓ the event is made to seem bigger than it really is;
✓ the worst is seen in the child and the situation all the time.

Success happens when:
✓ there are clear instructions;
✓ there is a small number of rules that the child knows;
✓ there are rewards that are achievable;
✓ there are routines;
✓ there are structures to the day;
✓ there are consistent approaches by both parents and teachers;
✓ the unimportant is ignored;
✓ there is an understanding with the child;
✓ arguments are avoided;
✓ there is time out for the child and yourself;
✓ the child is rewarded for gains, however small.

7   The Primary School Child

The primary school child may still have many of the same difficulties that he had when he was younger. At this stage the skills gap may be widening between the child and his peer group. Children who were slower because of lack of environmental stimuli will now mostly have caught up. At this stage there is an expectation that the child should have gained some of the basic skills required for reading, writing and ball games, for example.

It may be useful to read through chapters 2 to 4 before reading this one, even if the child is now at junior school level.

The junior school child with co-ordination difficulties may still not be able to dress and undress independently. His ball skills may also be poor. Eating neatly at table may still present a problem. The child's handwriting may still be at a very crude stage. It may be quite difficult for others to interpret his writing and his style of drawing may be more in line with that of a child one or two years younger.

STARTING AT PRIMARY SCHOOL

Difficulties that the child may face:

- Remembering the names of the teachers.
- The layout of the school, including the toilets.
- The daily routine.
- New children.
- Adapting to busy, noisy classrooms.
- Coping in the playground.
- Being set work that he has to get on with on his own.

- Lunchtime and breaktime.
- Negotiating PE and changing for this lesson.
- The rules of the school.

The first day at primary school can be very stressful. The child needs to deal with new situations that may be unfamiliar to him and the change may cause him great anxiety. Up to now he may have spent only part of the day away from a parent, and has often been in a small group. He now has to cope with a larger social group and negotiate all the rules that the school enforces. He no longer has his parents by his side for most of the day.

The rules may be implicit and not stated and this may cause him problems. He has to cope with the longer school day and may consequently become very tired. He will have to concentrate from the time he enters the school gates to the time he leaves. He is also trying to cope in different settings around the school—in the class, in the gym, and in finding the toilet.

PE. During the day the child may have to dress and undress for PE. This may make him feel under pressure. Not only does he have to prepare for the PE class; he has to do this in a certain time, keeping up with the rest of the class. At home he may still receive a lot of help from a parent in getting dressed. Once changed, he must then go along to the gym class and try to keep up with his peers. He may well find this difficult and stressful. If he is expected to practise ball skills or to climb up on to apparatus, he may find this hard and disorientating. He may well have very poor body awareness. After the lesson he has to repeat the process of dressing and return to his classroom. He may well find when he arrives back at the class that he feels unsettled and anxious because of his experience in the previous hour. It may take him ten to fifteen minutes to settle down again, and this will have an impact on the lesson as well.

Prepare for class changes

✓ Make sure his clothes are clearly marked so that he can identify them easily.
✓ Velcro on shoes and shirts, and elasticated cuffs and trousers, will speed up the process.

✓   He could go to school with PE kit *under* his clothes.
✓   Let the teacher know that he cannot manage certain items of clothing.

Lunch at school offers new challenges. It may be the first time the child has had to eat a meal in front of other children and away from his parents' guidance and support. He may have to pour a drink for someone else, or eat with a knife and fork. These may well be tasks with which he has continuing problems. He may try to rush his meal or not bother to eat at all, for fear of spilling his food. He may also be anxious about drinking too much in case he may need to go to the toilet urgently.

Tips
✓   A packed lunch can sometimes be the answer—negotiating a sandwich is easier than stew, for example.
✓   Prepacked drinks with a straw will be easier to drink and harder to spill.
✓   Remember a small packet of wet wipes in his bag to do a quick clean-up.
✓   If he has traditional school lunches, ask if he can sit near the teacher to begin with, who can help with pouring drinks and so on.

TOILETS

1 Getting there

Negotiating the school toilets may cause great concern. There are several stages in the process that may result in problems, the first being getting to and from the classroom. Direction is often a problem, and the child may lose his way there and back and take more time than expected, causing the teacher to be angry on his return.

2 Getting undressed

The second stage in going to the toilet is getting undressed and undoing buttons and zips. The child may have new trousers which are difficult to undo, and be in a hurry to go to the toilet. This may be the cause of an accident, which will be obvious to all on his return.

3 The wiping bit

If he needs to open his bowels and wipe his bottom, this may be an additional problem. He may forget to do this altogether, or he may not wipe completely. He may then return to the classroom smelly and the object of ridicule.

4 The stress

This can be one reason why some children avoid going to the toilet at all during the school day, and even end up having accidents. Some children become constipated, holding it in until they get home. Instead of concentrating on their lessons they are spending their time thinking about going to, or avoiding, the toilet. They may well complain of stomach-aches as well.

At a stage where he is trying to attain new skills alongside his peers, these added problems can cause great anxiety for the child. Many of these tasks put added pressure on a child who is trying to make friends.

Tips to help

✓ Make sure he can pull his trousers up and down easily.
✓ Give him a small packet of wet wipes to keep in his pocket.
✓ Make sure he knows where the toilets are in the school before he starts.
✓ Let the teacher know of his difficulties, and that he may need to go to the toilet at short notice.
✓ If he is having frequent accidents, make sure the teacher has a spare pair of pants in school.

Stephen's experience
'Where have you been, I thought you had got lost down the toilet?' said Stephen's teacher in a friendly manner, but in front of the class of eight-year-olds.

When Stephen got home he told his mother how he had been very upset at school because he had got lost and had felt frightened. He hadn't wanted to come back to the lesson, because he thought he might be told off. The worst thing of all, he felt, was being shown up in front of his peer group.

PROBLEM AREAS (see chapter 2 for explanations)

Fine motor co-ordination

Between the ages of five and eleven the fine motor movements of most children should become more refined, enabling them to use cutlery and to write. However, poor fine motor control may still affect the following functional areas:

Pencil grip
The child may still not have developed a tripod grip, or the grip may vary as he becomes more tired. He may try to apply pressure through the page to gain stability. If you watch him you may see him adopting awkward postures to try to improve his skills. The need to concentrate so hard to achieve a good level of handwriting

means that he cannot listen to what else is going on in the class-room. If his peers try to talk to him, even in a friendly manner, this may irritate him.

✓ Try different tools to encourage him to colour, paint and draw: a 'vibrating pen', a giant pencil—anything that he fancies.

✓ Practise screwing and unscrewing bolts and screws. Make a game with this, using dice and a timer to see how fast it can be done. Use lots of different sizes.

✓ Play with Stickle Bricks or Lego to help with manipulation.

✓ Practise warm-up hand exercises before he starts to do any writing.

✓ Practise making shapes using a peg board and pegs.

✓ Increase hand strength through using clay, rolling out 'snakes', and making shapes.

Handwriting
This may still appear very crude to the child, his teacher and his peer group. He may find it difficult to write along a line and may well go over the line, or run words into each other. The character of his letter formation will vary from one word to another and not show a consistent form. His handwriting may be better at the top of the page than the bottom and his ability to write may be better in the morning than the afternoon as he becomes more tired.

The 'grip' he uses to write may not necessarily be the tripod grip which is the most stable, and he may change his grip as he moves across the page. He may use his right hand for some activities and his left for others and not show a preference for one

side (laterality). He may change his posture as he writes across the page and may find difficulty crossing the midline. This means going across an imaginary line drawn down the centre of the body. When he is sitting down at a desk, this will mean he cannot write across a page. He may also not know where to start on the page.

✓ Try an alternative grip, holding the pen between the second and third fingers.
✓ There are several kinds of pen grips on the market. They are not always the answer—you may need to try a few. Different pens with 'grippers' on them may make writing easier for the child.
✓ Practise handwriting skills at a separate time from creative writing. The two skills do not need to be practised at the same time.

Musical instruments

Learning to play the recorder may be hard. It usually requires the child to stand up and place his fingers in the correct holes and also breathe properly while reading the music. Any one or all of these tasks may be a problem.

✓ Make sure the child is sitting comfortably.
✓ Place the music at the right height for the child. It will be harder for him to find his place again if he has to look down.
✓ Think about drums instead, or another percussion instrument that allows the child to sit.

Cutting

The child may still find it hard to use scissors. Placing his fingers in the holes and being able to co-ordinate the 'open and close' movement required may be hard for him to do as well as holding the paper with the other hand.

✓   See pp. 72–6 for advice on scissor skills.

Using a ruler
Holding a ruler while drawing with the other hand may also be
hard for the child to do. The ruler tends to move around and the
line ends up wobbling across the page.

✓   Use a ruler with a handle or ridge along it. There are metal
      ones available.
✓   Try a roller ruler.
✓   Place some Dycem on the end of the ruler to stop it slipping,
      or some Blu-tack.

Bilateral integration

This means moving both sides of the body together and bringing
hands in to the midline position. Using a knife and fork or being
able to draw or write may remain hard tasks for the child to do.
Children start to have bilateral integration while lying in the cot
and bringing their hands into the midline, and writing also
requires mastery of this skill.

Laterality

The child may still not have developed laterality. He will not be
better with one hand but may well be poor with both.

✓   Practise using left and right hands. Make catchers from a
      juice bottle—the larger the size, the easier it is to catch.
      Mark one to be held in the right hand with red tape and one
      for the left hand with blue. Get the child to catch with the
      hand that you call out.
✓   Play games—running to the right and to the left.
✓   Talk about right and left when out driving in the car. Ask the
      child which way he is going now, so that he develops an
      awareness of direction.
✓   Use language to link direction—'turn right at the castle,
      then left at the school'. This is easier than 'take the first right
      and second left'. The child can help you spot when you need
      to turn and then tell you whether that was right or left.

Gross motor co-ordination

As explained on p.28, gross motor skills enable us to balance and walk and run and catch and throw balls. For the primary school child, poor co-ordination in the following areas will assume greater importance:

Ball skills
The child may find *kicking a ball* difficult and may not be able to aim it accurately. He may kick too hard or too gently, and may lack the ability to grade his movements. To others watching they may seem crude.

✓   Try using a large foam ball which is easier to see and kick and moves more slowly.
✓   You can buy a ball on elastic, which can be attached to the child's waist.
✓   A football goal gives the child a large area to aim for.

Crawling, running and rolling and standing on one leg
You may see the child wobbling and appearing very unstable. He may also show movements of his arms and some mouthing movements as he tries to compensate for his instability. Improving hip stability will help this.

✓   Practise crawling races over and under obstacles.
✓   Trampolining helps with balance. Rebound therapy uses 'bouncing' techniques with trained therapists to help with co-ordination and social skills.

Walking downstairs or along a wall
Most children like walking along a wall, having their hands held, and will run downstairs with ease. The primary school child may exhibit fear and refuse to walk along a wall at all. If he is watched walking down the stairs, he may appear anxious and may hold on to the banisters, taking each step one at a time rather than walking down one step with one foot and the next step with the other.

✓   The child may need to have his eyes checked by a behavioural optometrist who will look at the function of the eyes. She will see whether the child can transfer from the black-

board to paper, or track an object or follow writing on a page. She will also see whether the child is long- or short-sighted.

Social skills

Some children may show signs of *frustration and anger*. The child usually does not exhibit this in school but may act it out when he gets home. Occasionally, however, he may lash out at other children around him. If he reacts in this fashion it may be for a number of reasons:

- He could have been bullied. He may have been called names or may have been physically bullied.
- In some instances it may even be because other children have sat too close to him while he is concentrating on other tasks. For example, if he is trying to achieve a task set by a teacher and also trying to shut out all the noises of the classroom, and another child starts nudging him, it may just be too much for him. He will then lash out. Seen in this context his behaviour is understandable. If you see only the end

point of this behaviour, the child will get told off for his actions.

✓   Let the child practise his social skills under supervision in a one-to-one situation at home so that he can then try to transfer them back into school.

✓   Start by limiting the time that a friend comes to play, to make sure it is a success.

Martin's story

Eight-year-old Martin was frequently placed in the 'punishment circle' in his school, for up to 40 minutes at a time, for the type of behaviour described above. He was told to stand still with his arms by his sides. Because of his posture, Martin had difficulty standing up correctly and it actually caused him discomfort. The teacher told him off for moving around, and he was then made to stay in the circle for extra time.

This is happening still, at the end of the twentieth century!

The child with co-ordination problems may appear quiet and withdrawn in school and be unable to relate well to his peers. In contrast to this behaviour, when he reaches the school gate he may 'fizz out'. Parents see him 'erupting' before he even gets as far as home. He may also have a tantrum in the car, demanding sweets or wanting to go swimming NOW, and refuse to be persuaded otherwise.

Take a snack along with you, such as a banana, when you meet your child. He may be feeling hungry and tired as well as stressed.

Tips to help

✓   Plan an after-school activity—a walk or a swim to give the child an opportunity to let off steam in a more controlled way.

✓   Give him even five minutes of protected time each day, which is his to have with you. This may be just sitting together and saying nothing, but he needs to know it is his time.

✓   Let the teacher know if his behaviour changes at home. An eye can then be kept on him at playtime, to watch where bullying may be occurring.

What does it feel like to have these problems?
Try walking around using a pair of binoculars turned round the wrong way. At the same time wear a pair of boxing gloves or thick gloves that are too big for you. Place a Walkman on your ears and then turn up the volume. Now walk around the room and around furniture and try to negotiate going up and down stairs. How difficult is this? Do you feel frustrated at your inability to do certain things? Do you want to just switch off the noise so that you can concentrate on getting down stairs or under the table? Try to get someone to talk to you at the same time. How do you feel now?

You can now understand just how these children feel by the end of the day with the problem areas described above.

The child will feel very *tired*, and *frustrated* by his poor output. He will be *angry with himself* because he wants to do better but is trying his hardest. He doesn't know how to try harder. He will be *angry with his peers* because he may have been treated with contempt and lack of understanding, and will feel *lonely* because he may have had no one to play with at playtime.

When he finally gets out of school all his frustration erupts and is directed at his parents. This is quite understandable when it is seen in context. Home is a safe place and it is safe to react.

Emotions
The child may still seem younger emotionally than other children of the same age. He will probably want attention and reassurance from the adults around him. He will work and behave much better in a one-to-one situation.

Visual discrimination

As with the pre-school child, 'busy' walls covered with paintings and drawings, and the movement of the other children around the class, may distract him from the task that he is trying to achieve.

Auditory discrimination

The child may be unable to filter out unnecessary sounds (see p.32).

Coping with change

All children like to know what they are doing and where they are going. This makes them feel more confident. A clear timetable works better in creating a structured environment.

Tips to help
✓ Timetables at home, in the school bag and by the back door will remind the child where and what he is doing.

Sequencing

Some children have a problem with sequencing, which will affect their ability to follow instructions, learn times tables or dress (see p.34).

✓ Picture stories help—the child has to place the pictures in the right order to tell a story.
✓ 'Simon Says' games are good for the child to practise following instructions.
✓ 'I went to the market and bought a . . .' is an easy game. You go round the group and everyone has to remember the list and add to it each time.

Perception

The child may have difficulty discriminating position in space. This can affect language—'top, bottom, in, out, on, before and after'. It can also affect vision and hearing.

✓ Jigsaw puzzles help develop perceptual skills (see p.32), gradually building up from very simple to more complex puzzles.

Additional tips to help (see also pp.37–9)
✓ Encourage him to work in smaller groups; he will have more chance of success.
✓ Reward effort, not just the result. After all, he is usually trying his hardest.
✓ Let him wear a watch with an alarm that can be set to remind him of work he needs to complete—but not a digital watch.

UNDERSTANDING TIME AND DISTANCE

Some children with dyspraxia, especially the children who didn't crawl, seem to have little or no understanding about the concepts of time and distance. They do not understand what time 'feels' like. When told to be ready in five minutes, they will still be sitting where you left them when the time is up. They may also stand in the shower for twenty minutes, not realising how much time has gone by.

Such a child needs to understand, first, what distance feels like, and second, what time feels like.

Activities to help

✓ Get the child to guess how many 'hands length' an object is, by using his hands or by watching you measure, for example, a table or a bed. Allow him to guess the distance and then allow him to feel the distance.

✓ Guess how many paces it is from one end of the room to the other, and then get him to pace it out.

✓ Move on to larger areas, such as strides of the length of the garden. Guess how many strides and then time how long it takes.

✓ Start to time how long it takes to do activities—guess first and then check.

✓ Use a timer to help.

✓ Use a timer to remind the child what a certain time feels like—for example halfway through homework, ten minutes in the bath.

✓ Talking alarm clocks are useful.

✓ Use a recorder that can tape about 15 seconds of messages.

✓ Get a watch with a buzzer, to remind the child that he needs to do something.

PERSONAL AND SELF-HELP SKILLS (see also chapter 4)

At this stage in their development many children with dyspraxia still require adult support and supervision when eating, drinking, dressing and undressing.

Eating and mealtimes

Mealtimes remain a huge problem for the child. Follow the advice
given on pp. 54–6.

Dressing and undressing

A child with co-ordination difficulties will still have several problems when dressing, including getting out of his clothes and with
the order in which they are put on. He may end up with shoes on
the wrong feet or his jumper on back to front. He may require help
and support at several stages in the dressing process.

Tips to help with dressing (see also pp.56–8)
✓   *Let him put out his clothes the night before,* arranged so that
     he can see the items he needs and the order in which to use
     them.
✓   *Make sure he is in a stable position* if he is putting on pants,
     socks or trousers. It is hard enough to put on a pair of socks,
     placing the heel in the right position, but if you have poor
     balance then you are already in a compromising position.
     Get him to sit on the floor.
✓   *Label clothes or use motifs* on the front to show which is the
     front and which the back.
✓   *The sequence of dressing* may need to be taught as well as
     the skills of putting on each item. Visual clues dotted about,
     showing what to put on and where it is, will help the child to
     gain confidence.
✓   *As well as placing clothes in the drawer* in the order he will
     put them on, use drawer dividers to make sure that things
     don't all fall into each other.
✓   *Have baskets on shelves.* This makes it easier to see where
     everything is.
✓   *Practise buttons and zips* with the garment off before
     putting the garment on. It will be harder for the child to do
     up fastenings out of sight, for instance at the back
✓   *Ties.* Put Velcro or elastic on the back of the tie, it will make
     it easier to get on and off. If you are teaching the child how
     to tie a tie, do this on yourself first and then on him.
✓   *Putting on his shoes.* 'Bunny lace' tying is the easiest
     method to teach. Use contrasting-coloured laces tied to each

other to make it easier to see. Make the first knot, tying one lace under the other. You can do this twice to hold it in position. Next make two bows (the 'bunnies') and tie a second knot with them. Try this off his foot before he tries it on his foot.

✓ *Use elastic laces, 'Bungy' or laces threaded through toggles.*

✓ *Put shoes on a foot mat with right and left marked.* The child could make this himself, by cutting out the shape of his foot and perhaps painting the two feet different colours—red for right and blue for left. When he takes his shoes off at night, he should place them on the foot mat, ready for the morning when he is in a rush for school.

✓ *Use trousers with elastic tops*, so they can be pulled up and down easily.

✓ *Help him get dressed for school* if you are in a hurry, and practise the skills he needs to gain when you are both less fraught. Weekends and holidays are a better time. When the child is tired, or when you are in a hurry, are not the times to tackle skills.

FATIGUE

Primary school children with co-ordination problems still suffer more from tiredness than others in their age group. Your child will have to focus more, both mentally and physically, and like the pre-school child will often work better earlier in the day than in the afternoon. When he gets home at the end of the day he may just want to collapse and do nothing. He does need to be paced at his own rate. After concentrating on an activity in the classroom, he may need to have time to run about. After this he will need time to settle down again before being able to attend in the classroom.

RIDING A BICYCLE

This requires skills of balance, bilateral integration and confidence. The child with depth perception problems will be frightened when going over surfaces that have different textures.

✓ Take the pedals off the bike and let the child sit on the bike and move it with his feet.

✓ Make sure the seat is low enough for him to do this.
✓ Let him take his feet off the ground for a few seconds.
✓ Practise pedalling on a three-wheeler first—he may try to pedal backwards rather than forwards.

DISLIKE OF CERTAIN TEXTURES OF FOOD, HAIR-BRUSHING AND NAIL-CUTTING

The child may dislike some textures of material next to his skin. For example, he may decide when he comes home from school to take off all his clothes. Or he may find having his nails cut or hair brushed causes pain. He may also dislike having his teeth cleaned. As a young child he may have preferred not to eat certain textures of food, and even now may have a very selective diet, preferring only certain foods and being unwilling to try others.

✓ Introduce different textures of food slowly alongside food he already likes. Stir in some texture to something smooth.
✓ If he likes ketchup with everything, let him use it when trying something new.
✓ You may find an electric toothbrush is better for him to use.
✓ Make up a 'feely' bag with different textures for him to feel—bubble wrap, foil, dry pasta shapes, velvet. Play a game and let him guess what they all are.

Mark's story
Mark is a warm and friendly but tense ten-year-old who is having some difficulties at school. Recently his school has decided that all pupils should wear a uniform. He constantly tells his mother it is 'itchy', and as soon as he gets home he just takes everything off.

His mother finds this a problem now as Mark wants to walk around the house with very little on, even when there are other people there. After some discussion with Mark, he has agreed that he will wear soft tracksuit pants and an old T-shirt as a compromise when he comes home.

OVERSENSITIVITY TO SOUND

Some children seem to be more sensitive than others to loud sounds. The young child may have become agitated when taken to a swimming pool. The echoing sounds may have been frightening. This same child is often frightened of fireworks, too. He will usually like the fireworks that look bright and colourful but will run indoors when it comes to the 'bangers'.

SLEEP DISTURBANCE

The child with DCD may be very restless in bed and not sleep well. If he has poor propioception then a light duvet may not give him adequate feedback to his body. See p. 62 for tips to help.

8 Bullying – What Can be Done?

Why should there be a chapter on bullying in a book about co-ordination problems? Because, unfortunately, most children with these problems will at some time in their lives have been or are currently being bullied. If you have been involved in this from any perspective—as the one who has been bullied, the parent or the teacher—you will understand how profound the effects can be on the child himself and those around him. This chapter discusses who gets bullied and why, and offers some ideas on what to do before, during and after the event.

ABOUT BULLYING

- Fifteen per cent of school-age children are involved as a victim or as the bullier.
- Boys are more likely to be bullied than girls.
- Boys bully in a more physical way.
- Girls tend to victimise the child they have chosen.
- In some schools today there is still an acceptance that this is just how it is, and a blind eye is turned and little done. In some schools the head teacher takes it very seriously and puts in place a whole school strategy, from the top down, to give the clear message that it will not be tolerated.

Who does it affect?

Bullying has a far greater impact than just on the person bullied and this needs to be considered when deciding what to do, in school and outside. It affects all of the following in some way:

- the bullied
- the bullier
- the school
- parents of both parties
- friends in and out of school

Who gets bullied?

The bullier seems to target the same type of individual every time. The child with co-ordination difficulties, by virtue of his appearance and actions, will certainly be at risk. Bullying can be both verbal and physical and can start from any age.

What type of child is bullied?

- The passive—those who are weak and feeble.
- The provocative—restless and irritable children; those with distractible behaviour.
- The physically weaker.
- Those with poor social skills who are less able to answer back.
- Those who lack interest in school.
- The child who may be school phobic—he is less likely to have a group of friends who can support him.
- Children who have overprotective parents.

As an adult, the child who has been bullied will remember exactly when and where the bullying took place. He may feel mistrustful towards other adults and may take a long time to become a fully confident individual. Unfortunately for some children, as adults they will have psychological problems and may show signs of depression that requires treatment.

These are generalisations, and many parents will not see why their child is being bullied. The child with co-ordination problems has a reason for being targeted that teachers need to be made aware of. It is more likely than not that he will be the victim.

What is the bullier like?

- He is usually persistent—once he sees success he will keep going.

- He himself may be insecure and feel he needs to become important.
- He may have good self-esteem and an overinflated opinion of himself.
- He has learnt that this is a method of control.
- He has watched his parents as his physical role models, and may have seen similar behaviour on TV and believe it to be acceptable.
- He may be bigger and stronger than his peer group, and become easily angered.
- He may start this behaviour in childhood and continue into adulthood.
- He may show aggression towards adults.
- He is seen by his peer group as tough.
- He may be average or below average in popularity and think that this will attract other children to him.

What are the parents of the victim like?

Some parents may be one of the following:

- *Overprotective* because of the problems they have with the child and their wish to keep him safe.
- *Caring*, wanting to make sure their child is kept with them.
- *Controlling*. They want to know where their child is and what he is doing at all times.
- They may not allow *conflict at home*, and may not show their children how to resolve their problems. It is a skill to know how to discuss a problem and reach a resolution and one that is often learnt around the dinner table.
- They may be *anticipating the problem* for their child, and then avoiding the situation and failing to reach a solution that will prevent him being bullied.

WHAT CAN BE DONE?

What you as a parent can do

- ✓ Tell the child not to hit back—this is not the answer.
- ✓ Act as a positive role model. Resolve conflict and don't let it simmer. How does your child see you behave with others —in the car, with people in shops, with work colleagues?

Have you learnt a positive style as an example for your child?

✓ Avoid verbal abuse and sarcasm towards your child.

✓ Reinforce caring and sensitivity to others.

✓ Be positive to the child—do you feel good about him? Do you say positive things about what he has achieved, or just point out his mistakes?

✓ Sometimes you have to accept a school change, and face the fact that matters have gone too far. Your child's self-esteem may have reached rock bottom.

✓ Your child may need time to talk about how he feels and learn to feel good about himself. He may have started to show deviant behaviour and you will need to seek counselling or psychological support.

What the school can do

✓ *Adopt clear-cut rules.* This is a top down approach to the problem, giving an unequivocal message to both teachers and pupils.

✓ *Provide a support network.* Nominate someone to whom the child can take his problems. A school counsellor for the pupils is one way of achieving this.

✓ *Check staff awareness.* Is there a training issue? Does the school need to make clear to the teacher how to recognise a child with co-ordination problems as he or she is one of the categories at higher risk of being bullied?

✓ *Identify likely candidates.* Prevention has to be better than cure. Establish who is vulnerable and then help the child with his social skills.

✓ *Co-operate with parents and work with them.* Work with the parent-teacher associations so that a strategy drawn up in school is known by the parents to help them out of school.

✓ *Use role-play or 'circle time'.* These are ways of discussing with other children the impact that bullying has not only on the child concerned, but on the class and the school.

✓ *Set up a mentoring or befriending scheme with an older child.* If this can be done, it provides a feeling of support and protection for the child, until he regains his confidence.

✓ The bullier will also need help and support to sort out his or her problems.

SIGNS OF A CHILD BEING BULLIED

- Torn clothes and damaged books.
- Unexplained bruises or scratches.
- Not bringing classmates home—if your child is a loner then he will be more at risk.
- No single best friend.
- Is he not being invited to parties?
- Is he reluctant to go to school?
- Illogical route to school. He may give a garbled explanation of why he has to take a long route to school—be suspicious of this.

What are the signs at home?

- Restless sleep and bad dreams.
- Losing interest in school and lowered grades. Deterioration in work is worrying if there are no clear reasons for it.
- Unhappy, sad or irritable.
- Stealing extra money.
- Loss of appetite.

What signs should be looked for in school?

- Called names, given orders by some children.
- Laughed at by his peer group or by older children.
- Shoved, pushed, and kicked in the playground.
- Books or money taken or damaged.
- Bruises or cuts, for which the child will give little or no explanation.
- The child who always seems to be on his own in the playground.
- The child who seems to want to stay close to a teacher at break time.
- The child last chosen for the team.
- The child who has difficulty speaking up in class.
- Distressed and tearful in class.
- Gradual or sudden deterioration in classwork may be an indicator of both fear and harassment that is taking place.

WHY ARE THESE CHILDREN BULLIED?

Children often choose the individual who is different from them. This may be the child with glasses, the one who is very tall or short, who has a speech impediment, or who is slower to react. The child with dyspraxia and related problems may look like one of these. He may appear slower to react, his appearance is not always neat and tidy, and he doesn't usually do well at sport. Boys are judged by their ability with the ball, whereas girls are often judged more on their work in the classroom. The child with both fine and gross motor problems will lose out on the sports field and in the classroom.

He will not be chosen to be in the 'gang', so will have less protection than other kids and be seen to be 'easier' picking. His classwork looks poor compared to his peers although he may actually be verbally able, which may be resented. For example, when it comes to general knowledge he may be very good, but he may shout out inappropriately in class and cause other children irritation. Some children may be more overweight as they are less active, and avoid games because of their lack of ability.

Key points to identify why the child with DCD may get bullied

- *Appearance*. His clothes may not be colour co-ordinated, buttons may be undone, shoelaces untied, and he may wear glasses.
- *Social skills*. He may have poor social skills and is often better playing with younger or older children.
- *Verbal dyspraxia*. His speech production may not be clear. He may be slower to express his thoughts.
- *Overweight*. Because of poor ability at sport he may avoid playing games and then turn to food for comfort. This combination means that some children will be overweight.
- *Seen as 'stupid'*. His peers see his work on the wall and may assume he lacks ability.
- *Immaturity*. Many children with co-ordination problems are less mature than others of the same age. This means they are less able to cope when they are bullied. The child may not be as quick to respond verbally and the bullier sees instant success.

- *School sports day*. This is the perfect day to be shown up in front of his peers. Being poor at running, not being able to do the egg-and-spoon or the dressing game, means that everyone, including parents, can identify the child with co-ordination problems!

HOW DOES IT FEEL TO BE BULLIED?

Thirteen-year-old Peter explains

It is difficult. My handwriting is bad and it makes me feel embarrassed when the teacher puts my work up on the wall. I have told him that I am trying my hardest but sometimes I am made to rewrite things all over again.

I try to make friends with other children in my school but they are mean to me. I get pushed sometimes and one boy called me 'a big fat pig'. I wouldn't give him any of my crisps, because I wanted to pay him back. My sister has lots of friends, and she is mean to me sometimes and says, 'Why can't you get friends?'

I can't do maths very well at the moment. My teacher wants me to use a compass and I don't do that very well. I wish they would talk more about things in class rather than writing it all down. I feel bored then, because I can't do the work the same as the others. I just wish I could leave school and go and work in a kennels. I love animals and my dog is the best thing I have.

Remember, the bully could be a teacher!

As a parent, how can you help?

✓ Talk to your child and give him time. If you have other children, give them each time with you that is exclusively theirs.

✓ Let him have time to wind down when he comes home from school. This may mean running around with the dog in the garden or slumping in front of the television, going for a swim or reading a book.

✓ There may be a club in your area for children with learning problems. Let your child see if he wants to go. He may not realise there are other children with similar problems who could give support to each other.

✓ Invite children home from school, but be around to supervise and help with play, especially with the younger child.

You may need to 'play' with them—a board game or card game or a cookery session. This will let your child make friends but feel supported. You can guide him out of a situation if he is behaving inappropriately. He may become overexcited or lose interest.

✓ Be aware of the signs of bullying—school avoidance, change in behaviour, sleep disturbance, appetite disturbance, and avoidance of some activities—and be ready to act.

If you are a teacher, let the child know that you understand he has difficulties and tell him that he can come to you if he is running into problems in the class or the playground.

9 Hobbies to Develop out of School

Any hobby that a child pursues out of school should be one that he has chosen and one that he enjoys. A lot of his time is taken up with activities he finds hard to complete, so his out-of-school activities should be ones that can not only help him but that he can look forward to doing every week.

Some ideas

Horse riding
This activity promotes stability. It also helps the child to balance and feel a rhythm. The child with low self-esteem can gain confidence and relate well to the horse—it does not judge him in any way. It is a good idea to choose riding schools that understand the needs of your child and will not expect him to gallop by lesson two! Some centres are tailored to 'riding for the disabled' and are more patient, allowing the child more time to gain the necessary skills and go at his own pace. The teacher may need to give visual as well as verbal instructions and show the child what is expected of him. The child may need a marker on the reins to say which is right and left, as direction could be a problem. Gloves with rubber grippers on the palm surfaces will help him hold the reins. Make sure that he has the correct footwear, otherwise it will make it even harder for him to grip properly.

Yoga
This is an activity for all age groups. It allows the individual to go at his own pace and is non-competitive. It helps with relaxation and to improve body awareness.

Swimming
This allows the child to strengthen both his upper and lower body. Play games with your child in the water—for example, throw quoits in and let him fetch them and then climb out of the water. Running races in the water will strengthen his legs. Using a float on working on the child's front will help to work on both legs and arms. *Let it be fun* and allow him to just play rather than work. He may need to learn with an instructor one-to-one. Some children find it easier to swim under (rather than on top of) the water first.

Cookery
Preparing food is a good way of promoting conversation and producing an end product the child can be proud of. It can help both fine and gross motor skills. Making pastry, for example, requires rolling, cutting, shaping and spooning. Making bread requires rolling, pouring and shaping the dough. Start with the last task first, so that the child sees an end point and doesn't lose concentration—for example, placing the jam in the jam tarts and then putting them in the oven. The child can see the end product ten minutes later.

Try a non-competitive hobby
Birdwatching, singing, sailing, judo or T'ai Chi can all be fun activities. The child is not seen to fail or pass at these when compared to his peer group.

Photography
An enjoyable way of being creative and showing others what your child can do. It may be more successful than drawing or painting. Consider using a Polaroid camera, which gives instant results. A video camera can also be good fun. Digital cameras allow the child (within minutes) to see on the computer screen what he has just taken.

Pottery
This is good for co-ordination and improving muscle tone. Start by making 'coil pots'. The child has to roll out 'snakes' and build the pot up with them. You can use the clay that does not need baking—you may need to soften it to make it easier to handle. Allow the child to decide what he wants to make, don't give him too much guidance.

Drama classes
Acting may help to develop confidence. It is good for improving social skills and gives the child an opportunity to express his frustrations and other feelings in a controlled way.

Trampolining
An activity that can help with posture and balance. It can also make the pelvic girdle more stable.

Canoeing
Consider choosing this water sport to begin with in preference to sailing. It will help balance and gross motor skills, especially the shoulder girdle.

Cubs and Brownies
The success of this is dependent on the individuals running the group. If they are sympathetic the child will benefit from the group activities and at the same time improve his or her social skills. It is worth telling the leader that your child may find certain activities hard do—for example, knots, football and writing lists. Rather than do those he may do better helping to organise or helping the leader.

Cycling

Quad biking is easier to do than riding a two-wheeler as it has greater stability. A tricycle or scooter can also be easier to use. There are attachments that can turn adult bikes into tandems, a choice that enables the child to join in with the rest of the family, provided he has the right equipment.

Badminton

Consider this as your first choice in racquet sports because the racquet itself is lighter and the shuttlecock moves more slowly. To start with you could make it even easier and use a large shuttlecock. Break up the skills required. Start by throwing the shuttle to the child and get him to hit it back to you. Then allow him to hit the shuttle against the wall. Only when he has mastered these skills should you encourage him to hit the shuttlecock over the wall.

Martial arts

T'ai chi, judo or karate all require self-control and discipline. They also require the child to follow a sequence of commands. You may need to remind the instructor to repeat these in small chunks. The benefit of these activities is on gross motor function, self-esteem and body awareness. The child can go at his own pace and the (constant) repetition of the work over the allotted time means that success can gradually be achieved.

Line dancing

This can be a good form of exercise for both the older child and the adult. It helps with social skills, co-ordination and self-esteem. When the child or adult joins a class, most of the others are in the same position (all new) and therefore he can gradually learn what to do, at his own pace.

Aerobics

This, too, may help the older child and the adult. Many classes follow the same pattern every week. If the individual remains at the back of the class he or she can not only go at his or her own pace but can also practise, week after week (at home and in class), until confidence is achieved.

Rambling and orienteering
Many children and adults like walking. This can be done with others if you join a rambling group. Walks are usually divided into different capabilities (based on time and distance), from a short walk to an arduous trek. It allows the individual to have an opportunity to meet others, and exercise at his own pace.

Astronomy
This is a hobby that others may not consider and could be the one that the child with co-ordination difficulties (and related problems) may enjoy. It is not dependent on good co-ordination and may give the child an area of expertise that could then be fed back into the classroom.

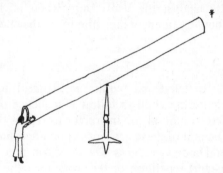

Chess
Some children with specific learning difficulties can become very good chess-players. They could join a club outside school and it gives them an opportunity to play with people at the same skill level, and not be totally related to age.

Computers
The child with co-ordination problems may have to learn to rely upon the computer to produce written work. This can be turned into an advantage, in that he may become very highly skilled and could consider this as an occupation for life.

10 The Secondary School Child

The difficulties that occur with secondary school children can be partly related to the age and stage they are at. All adolescents have to go through both physical and emotional changes. For many this roller coaster is hard enough but with other problems on top of this it can be a time when behavioural problems emerge as well.

The adolescent may have had a difficult time and have struggled through junior school. His self-esteem may now be at an all-time low and the stress of moving to a larger school may bring a new set of problems for him. He may still have fine motor control difficulties that affect his handwriting, and the social difficulties that he had when younger may be even greater at this time, when peer group acceptance is under pressure and so crucial to the way a teenager feels.

He may feel that education has failed him and that teachers don't understand that he has been trying his hardest over the years. He may start to feel that it is not worth trying and want to show his frustration through disruptive behaviour in school as well as at home.

WHERE DO THE PROBLEMS OCCUR, AND WHY?

One of the main difficulties that the child first has to overcome is change, which is often hard for the teenager with dyspraxia and related problems.

Change

When the child moves from primary to secondary school he has to cope with new surroundings which may be much bigger than he is used to. He has to get to know his teachers. His new class may include children he has not known before. By the end of the second or third week, most children without problems will have settled down and be familiar with their surroundings. But the child with co-ordination problems may continue to be late for class and feel very disorientated for quite some time.

He may take time to get to know the layout of the school and need to be taken around for a while until he has got his bearings. Class sizes may be bigger than he is used to, which then in turn means more noise and more movement. For the child who is easily distracted by noise or movement, this can bring an added dimension to his problems.

How you can prepare the child

✓ *Plan*. Obtain a layout of the school before the child starts the term. This can be pinned up in his room to help him become familiar with it.
✓ *Visit*. Try to visit the school more than once and look at some of the key classrooms that will be used by the child. He also needs to know where he will keep his belongings. Ask if you can go along as well so that you can help him, as you will know where problems are occurring. You may be thought of as a nuisance, for parents of secondary school children are often kept at more of a distance than in primary school.

✓   *Photograph.* Take some photographs of the rooms—and of teachers if they will allow it. You could make a map and label the rooms and then stick the pictures of the personnel on it, so that the child can learn these before the start of the term.

✓   *Timetable.* If the school can give you the timetable, place it in the child's room, downstairs and in his bag, so he can easily prepare for the following day.

✓   *Gain previous reports and information, and talk to the teachers.* Let the school see any reports before the start of term, and discuss the implications. Let the school have any additional information about the problems so that they can be fully informed.

✓   *Prepare clothes for school and practise changes in and out of them.* Have some practice sessions with your child so that he can dress and undress quickly. You will then see what help is required before the start of term.

✓   *Suitable shoes.* Use shoes that can be put on and taken off independently, or adapt them.

✓   *Make clothes easy.* Adapt them if necessary—but remember that your child will want to look like his friends. He will prefer to walk around with his shoelaces undone than to wear 'funny' laces.

✓ *Meet other children beforehand.* During the holidays, ask over to your home children who will be in your child's class, and arrange to meet up with one or two children ten to fifteen minutes before school starts on the first morning, so that the child has someone else to go in with. If you know of an older child, see if she will keep an eye on your child and guide him around at break times for the first few days.

Why are there problems?

Youngest in the school

In primary school your child will have been one of the oldest in the school and will have been able to play with younger children. Sometimes he may have been thought of as a helper. In reality he may actually have found the play of a child even two or three years younger than himself to be more appropriate, both at an emotional and at a physical level.

Once he has moved to senior school he no longer has the younger children around and he himself is now the youngest. This can expose his social weaknesses. His difficulties in keeping up with his peers now become more obvious. Conversation between teenagers is fast and furious and the need to keep up and respond not only appropriately, but with wit as well, may be too much for him. He may find that he retreats away from the group, especially when his peers actively exclude him because he is seen as 'different'.

✓   Encourage friends to come home, so that they can practise his social skills in a protected environment.

✓   If he wants to play the sort of games that younger children play, let him do so. He may still have younger friends outside school, so let him mix with them as well. He still needs this sort of social activity.

Coping socially

Being popular and sociable is one of the most important things for teenagers: it gives them 'street-cred'. Some children with co-ordination difficulties have a problem with this. Your child may still not always have a clear understanding about social distance and may stand too close to his peers. Most of us have an in-built feeling about how far we should stand or sit next to someone, but this does not always seem to have been acquired in these children.

The feedback from the child's peer group will be poor as other children begin to shy away from him and feel he is 'odd'. He may also give too much or too little eye contact, interrupt a conversation inappropriately, or break off and walk away in the middle of someone else talking. He seems to have poor social grading alongside poor motor grading. He may still be very dependent on his parents and may seek to hold hands when out or try to sit on his parent's lap. Other children of a similar age would have decided by this stage that it was not seen as 'cool' and would prefer only to have close contact while at home.

THE CHALLENGES OF THE WORK

Basic skills and beyond

At primary school there is time devoted to acquiring the basic skills needed to learn a subject. Periods for times tables, handwriting and reading are allowed in the school curriculum. When the child moves to secondary school he is supposed to have acquired these skills to a reasonable standard. There is little time for practice at secondary stage, as speed is essential. The child with co-ordination problems may still have poor handwriting and if other methods for recording his work are not considered he may be disadvantaged. He may be seen as slow, lazy, or untidy. He may be given back work to do again and again, because it is seen as messy. The child usually has tried his hardest on each occasion. Repeated punishment only serves to demoralise rather than encourage this child.

More subjects

The child at secondary school also has to cope with more subjects and more teachers. In primary school the teacher may have got to know the child well and have understood his difficulties. The move to a big school makes it harder for teachers to get to know him well. They may only see him for a short time each week. Some teachers may have little specialist knowledge about DCD and dyspraxia and will regard the child as a malingerer rather than one who is struggling and having a problem.

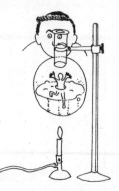

New subjects such as chemistry bring fresh challenges. Posture and balance may already be compromised, and now the child has to try to balance on a 'bar stool' while pouring chemicals into a small container. The poor balance, added to poor fine motor skills, could make this not just a challenge for the child, but a potentially dangerous situation.

THE ORGANISATIONAL SKILLS REQUIRED

At secondary school the child is faced with having to become more self-reliant and less guided by the teacher. He is no longer in one classroom with one teacher for most of the day, but now has to get from class to class with books and equipment. In addition he needs to do this in reasonable time and also to remember to have the relevant equipment for the class he is attending. This can be particularly difficult for the child with co-ordination problems. He may forget the same ruler or book week after week, and the teacher may come to think this is a deliberate act. It may, however, be related to the fact that his previous class was PE, for example, and the child has been left feeling flustered and disorientated. He will be the one to arrive five minutes late, missing the first part of the lesson and the instructions, and will end up being confused.

By simple strategies these children can be helped to become more organised. They need to start this before they leave for school in the morning and must continue to be organised before they go to bed, ready for the next day.

As well as not remembering all the equipment, the child may forget to put his homework in his bag, get home and not remember what has been asked of him. He then returns to school the next day and gets into more trouble for not doing his homework.

The disorganisation is also linked to a lack of awareness of time. He may still have no sense of what time feels like. For example, at exam time he does not recognise when he should be halfway through an exam paper. At home he may not understand how long he has been in the bathroom.

Improving organisational skills

Tips to help
✓   *Timers*. As with a younger child, use an egg-timer when he is working at a piece of homework, and set it every fifteen

minutes to remind him what this 'feels' like. Place the timer out of his vision, so that it does not become an added distraction. A timer in the shower or bathroom, set for ten minutes, will act as a reminder when his time is up.

✓ *Digital watch*. These are often easier to read than a traditional watch and can be set to ring at certain times to remind the teenager to complete a particular activity.

✓ *Buzzer key reminders*. All sorts of reminder key rings and pens can be used. There are available both a pen with a rewinding tape and a key ring that can record about 15 seconds of tape. They can be useful in just saying, 'Remember the German book', for example, and can be played back at home to check the books into the bag again to go back to school.

✓ *Laminated timetable*. This can be put up in the child's room to remind him to get out the appropriate clothes and sports kit for the following day. Another copy can be on the inside of his school bag and a third one in his locker, acting as a reminder at key points during the day.

✓ *Key on a chain*. Losing a locker key is a problem when it happens more than once. Putting it on a string around the child's neck may be dangerous. Using a key ring on a plastic 'curly' chain means it is where he will need it. If his trousers don't have a belt loop, sew a piece of tape inside a pocket for the key ring to be attached to. Make sure you also have a spare key for emergencies.

✓ *Mentor or buddy*. Adjusting to a new school is very stressful. A buddy or friend who knows his way around can make all the difference. He can take the child from class to class. He can also remind him to check his books into his bag at the end of the day, and help him to make sure he has the correct equipment for each class. This may become a problem if the other children think that the child is having extra help all the time, and it needs to be handled sensitively to make sure the child doesn't become a target for bullying as a consequence.

An older child as a mentor, perhaps someone in the sixth form, can also be very supportive. He will know the rules of the school, and where difficulties are likely to arise. He can also sometimes sort out a problem quietly and discreetly. The sixth-former can talk to the class teacher if help is needed, whereas the child may be reluctant to do so, especially if he is new to the school.

✓ *Wet wipes in bag for toilet.* Toileting may still be a real problem and the child may be smelly as a result. Packing a small pack of wet toilet tissues means he can easily and discreetly clean himself if he needs to go to the toilet in school. From the beginning, it is important that he knows where the toilets are, and the teacher should be told that he might need to go more often. Adapted clothing should be used to make it easy for him to get undressed quickly—for example slightly bigger trousers that can be pulled down.

✓ *Appropriate clothing—labelled, and in drawers that are labelled.* At home make sure the child is well prepared for the day. Drawers should be ordered and labelled in a way that makes it easier and logical to find clothes. The child should be part of the process of organising this, as this will reinforce for him where items are.

✓ *Pencil case.* Use a clear plastic pencil case so that the objects can be seen from the outside. A list of the contents can then be stapled on the inside, but facing the outside of the case. At the end of the lesson all the items can be checked backed into the case. This reduces the chances of losses.

✓ *Use a ruler with a ridge* or an architect's metal ruler with a handle, to make it easier to place the ruler on the paper. Put Dycem on the end of the ruler so that it grips to the paper.

✓ *A selection of pens* and pencils with and without grips should be tried out to see what suits the child. There are some pens with a rubber area to grip on to that can be quite comfortable. The child with ligamentous laxity may find that a gripper makes it harder, not easier to use, and he may need a 'cuff' made from Neoprene to stabilise his hand.

✓ *Make sure there is a spare set* of all equipment which stays at home so that the school pencil case can stay in the child's bag ready for the following day.

✓ *Use scissors* that are the appropriate size for the child, and if he is left-handed, get left-handed scissors. If he cannot use scissors well, think about using artist's cutters or dress-maker's scissors (Peta roll-cut scissors) which may be easier to manipulate, or even try battery-operated scissors.

✓ *Have a homework diary* that can be checked in and out, with the timetable clearly written on the inside cover.

EXAM TIMES

Exams can be an added stress for any child with learning difficulties, but particularly for the child who may be trying to concentrate and who becomes easily distracted by sounds and movement around him.

He may need to have extra time allowed to get his ideas down on paper, or to be placed in another room away from others, or the use of an amanuensis who will take down the words the child has dictated. However, for some children extra time may not be the answer but may just extend the agony.

Some children have difficulty understanding the concepts of time. This may be a problem at this time when they need to be able to pace themselves and must plan and organise their work within a time-frame. The use of digital watches and a clock on the desk in front of him can help (see p.101 for further ideas).

Study skills

All children need to be prepared for exams to be successful. The child with organisational difficulties, poor handwriting and poor concepts of time faces more problems than most. He requires forward planning to make sure that he feels prepared for the day.

When considering working for an exam or test, it is necessary to think about how you gather in information and then get it out again:

- *Input*. Information comes from reading books, the teacher talking, class discussions, videos, film outings, observation, and making and doing things. It is absorbed through all the senses—what you see, hear and feel, and even what you taste.
- *Storage*. Information has to be processed and understood, which requires thinking, organising, remembering and then planning. It is then necessary to store this information so that it can be retrieved when it is wanted.
- *Output*. When it has to be retrieved, knowledge can be shown by telling it or writing it down, or even by acting it out. Difficulties in studying may occur at the input, processing or output stages for the individual with organisational difficulties and problems with concentration. If sound or movement easily distracts him he may find it harder to concentrate and listen in class. It may also be harder for him to take down the information in time. Once it is taken down it may not be fully understood and not properly stored. Imagine typing work into a computer—you can see it all in front of you. You forget to press the 'save' button. When you switch on the computer again, it is no longer there.
- *Motivation* plays an important part in learning.

What affects learning?
- *The setting*. Is it a nice room looking out over gardens, or is it cold and draughty?
- *The people* you are with. Are you with your friends and enjoying yourself or are you in a room full of strangers?
- *Prior learning experiences*. Have they been good or bad?
- *The teacher*. You want to please her because you like her style of teaching.

- *A means to an end*. You need to pass the examination to get to college.
- *Other distractions*. You have had to give up something else you like to be there—for example, football.

Why do individuals fail examinations?
- Not taking in the information to learn from.
- Not taking the time to learn and relearn.
- Poor understanding.
- Poor writing—can't be read by the examiner on the notes from the term can't be read.
- Wrong material learnt.
- Don't see the importance or relevance of the examination so don't want to bother to try.

Study skills and preparing for the examinations

If you are a parent reading this, let your child read it as well, it is aimed at him.

For some people, knowing what to do and doing it can be two different things, and it may take a lot of failure for some to accept the need to change. It usually means that the person has to have a very clear reason for doing so.

Planning for the exams or work in term time
✓ Create a timetable several weeks before the exam. Decide when and where you are going to study and the length of each session. Regular studying will pay greater dividends than a 'blast' at the end.
✓ Plan to include relaxation and exercise time as well. You will study better if you have had some exercise.
✓ Do you work better to music or in silence? Is your room too warm, so that you feel like dropping off to sleep after half an hour?
✓ Too much coffee and tea is not the best way to keep you alert. Shorter intensive work periods are better than hours and hours of 'pretend' studying.
✓ Don't study for more than one hour at a time. It is not the amount of time you study, but how effective you are.
✓ Try to understand what works for you. If you have good visual memory, pictures, maps, and cards may be the right

route. If you have a good auditory memory it may be better to use a tape recorder and make 'notes' in this way.

✓ Give yourself a goal to reach each week and if you reach it, reward yourself with a treat.

✓ Every week look at the long-term timetable, and in addition write out a weekly one with your objectives.

✓ Consider working in a group or with a partner occasionally, but goals need to be set, and the time decided upon, otherwise it can easily turn into a party!

Tips for the student before the exams

✓ Use several methods to learn—recite aloud, write notes, record, and change into note form, try to visualise your work on the page. Use mnemonics to remind yourself of a list of items.

✓ Obtain a copy of the notes from another student to learn from.

✓ Get hold of old test papers and practise them, to understand the style of the exam and the type of answers expected.

✓ Go through the questions and highlight the key words and how they want you to answer them. If you don't understand, go through them with your teacher.

✓ Test and retest yourself—make notes, expand them, and contract them into shorter phrases to remind you. Learn one area, move on to another area, go back and check you have remembered the first one. Check this again several days later to reinforce the information.

✓ Try to think of ways to remind you of details—draw pictures, outline in different-coloured pens.

✓ Use a highlighter to outline key passages you need to understand. To do this you need to read it carefully

✓ If there are revision books available for the subject, look at these, they often have reminders and short cuts to learning.

✓ There are CD Roms and tapes available—consider other methods of learning.

✓ Go and see the play you are studying, or the local castle. It is easier for some individuals to learn visually.

✓ Look on the Internet for your subject area.

✓ Keep calm. Try a relaxation technique. The more anxious you get the less able you are to concentrate on what you need to achieve.

The exam

✓ Prepare your bag for the next day with all your pens and equipment you need.

✓ Get a good night's sleep. Have a warm bath, read a book, but don't study through the night. If you are too tired you will not be able to think clearly.

✓ Have breakfast—you will concentrate better if you do.

✓ When you get to school, don't listen to all the other chatter —they may sound as if they know more than you, but they probably don't.

✓ In the exam, when you turn over the paper, give yourself five minutes to read through it and underline key words. Plan an essay or passage of writing—show this outline if you don't manage to complete it.

✓ Check to see when you are halfway through the exam time and see where you are. This may make a difference to how you answer other questions—if necessary do it in note form if you haven't enough time to finish.

✓ Leave time to check your work at the end.

✓ Relax afterwards—you cannot do anything about it when it's over.

✓ If you fail, consider why, and what you need to change—is there another way of reaching your goal? You may need to think about going to a college and doing an access course, or consider working and a day release course. Don't give up. Learn from this. Ask others their opinion.

How can parents help?

For most parents, examination times can be a great worry. How much should you push your child? What help should you be giving him? Supporting your child and being there with him or her is one of the key things. He needs to know that if he fails you will still accept him for what he is, and not for what he has done. You may need to think of a strategy to follow if he does fail and what alternatives exist in the area for him. Is it better for him to re-sit, or is there a more practical alternative to enable him to reach his goal?

Tips to help

✓ Encourage your child.

✓ Provide the right environment for learning and the right tools. Make sure there is a spare set of pens, pencils and so on.

✓ Look for study aids at the library and in the shops to help with his coursework.

✓ Look out for plays to go to and take him to the local art gallery or science museum

✓ Offer to help with the organisation of the work—you could offer to help make clear cards with brief notes on them.

✓ You may need to transcribe tapes for your child into easy-to-read notes.

✓ Be available to test and discuss with your child.

✓ If you are unsure of the content of the work, speak to his teacher.

✓ Make sure your child has adequate rest and eats regular meals.

How can the teacher help?

The child with DCD and dyspraxia may need to learn in a different way from other children in the class.

Tips to help

✓ Give an overview of the topics covered for the term so that your pupil can see where his learning fits in.

✓ You may need to use a variety of techniques to help the pupil—tapes, photocopied sheets, group work and discussion to help him.

✓ Summarise at the start of the lesson what you will teach and at the end what you have taught.

✓ Make sure the pupil has a homework diary and check it for him. Buddy him up to another pupil whom he can ring to check on homework. He is still likely to forget his books.

✓ Make sure you have spare sets of pens and so on, in case he arrives for the exam without them.

✓ Let the student have another pupil's notes to learn from.

✓ Help the student construct a timetable for learning.

✓   Explain what is expected from the exam and the format in
    which it should be written.
✓   Write these instructions down as well.

11 Boosting Self-esteem and Improving Social Skills

When some children with co-ordination difficulties try to make friends, the way they act may set up a stream of responses that makes any growth in friendship difficult. The child gets off to a bad start and lacks the ability to rectify the situation. Often he is poor at grading his movements, but his attempts at being sociable may be equally poor. How does a child choose his friends? Why do we select one person rather than another to go and talk to in a crowd? What is it that makes you avoid someone, and not even give that person a chance to show you what he or she is really like?

The DCD child displays a lack of certain skills that will make it harder for him. These are a few reasons:

- *He is different.* If your child is very sensitive, or more mature than his peer group, or very gifted in one area, he will stand out and be seen as different from others. His responses in a social situation may not conform with those of his peer group, or of adults he is addressing. He may not be able to change his style to adapt to different situations. For example, children talk to their friends differently from the way they address their parents and other adults. The child with dyspraxia and related problems may not distinguish between the two: he may be overfamiliar with an adult, and not understand when he is told off. His intention was not to be cheeky, but it will be misinterpreted.
- *Appearance.* A mismatch of clothing which is not in line with others.
- *Personality.* He may be shy or too outgoing. He may feel

unable to interact with others and respond quickly in a group
setting. He may react too quickly in a situation and go over-
board, being overenthusiastic.

- *He may continue to talk for too long* or at too high a volume.
- *Social distance.* He may sit too close and give too much eye
  contact to the person he is addressing.

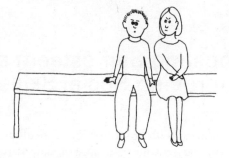

Social mistakes that the child may make

- *Acting as a know-all* when he has acquired some informa-
  tion and telling everyone else about it, not realising when he
  should keep it to himself.
- *Passing on secrets* that have been told in confidence, not
  understanding what was being asked of him.
- *Getting into a fight*, and being unable to resolve the situation
  easily.
- *Being persistent* with a wish or demand, after others have
  moved on in the conversation.
- *Constant interruptions* when others are talking.
- *Becoming angry* or upset when he fails.
- *Becoming overly excited* when he is winning.
- *Talking too much*—on and on and on.
- *Not being willing to share* with others.
- *Being too direct and blunt*—for example, drawing attention
  to some aspect of another person's appearance.
- *Not knowing how to start or stop* a conversation or leave a
  group.

How you can help your child improve his social skills

Model the behaviour you want to see
There is no better way for your child to learn than to follow the way you interact with others. Your behaviour will allow him to observe good social skills and to learn them from you, in a protected environment. It is also useful for him to watch others and be shown what is inappropriate. Use the television or videos to show him this. Allow him to tell you what he thinks is right or wrong, so that he becomes more aware of what good social skills look like.

Tips to help

✓ Explain to your child about social distance—an elbow's width sitting next to someone and an arm's length if he is standing in front of you are two simple measures you can teach. You don't need to think about this but he will need to be taught.

✓ Check on eye contact—does he look at someone when he is talking to them either not at all or too much? Try to practise this with him at home. You may need to give him a visual reminder such as a signal that he recognises—for example, tapping your hand if you want him to look at someone.

✓ Does he let others know that he is listening to them with

nods of the head, or with 'mms' and 'yeses', etc.? If he doesn't, he needs to understand that others will think he doesn't care what they are saying.

✓ Practise starting and ending a conversation with him. Pick a topic or hobby he enjoys.

✓ Let him have a few stock topics he can pick on—holidays, TV programmes, computer games—that his peers will also be talking about.

✓ Tell him when he has behaved inappropriately. You will need to be explicit and say what he said and why it was wrong and what he could do to improve the way he handled a situation for the next time. Do it at a time when you are both relaxed and he will be more likely to be receptive.

Practise the behaviour

Let your child practise with close family members who will be more lenient if mistakes are made. It must be agreed that they will not laugh at him practising, otherwise any benefit will be dashed immediately, and it will be harder for him to try again. They should not criticise him, but praise his efforts.

Feeling good

Good social skills stem from confidence in ourselves. If your child has been bullied, he will feel bruised and battered psychologically, and will require building up again.

Tips to help
✓ Praise effort, not output.
✓ Appreciate how hard he is trying.
✓ Praise his creativity.
✓ Tell others in front of him how pleased you are.
✓ Say it and show it.
✓ Keep encouraging your child, even for small efforts.

Practise in the 'real' world

When he has gained confidence, let him join a club or activity that he fancies. He will have a topic to talk about which will help to launch him into the new social setting. It is also a test to see if he can make friends and keep them successfully. Bear in mind that he may fail and then need building up again.

Check the level of success
Talk to your child when he has been to school, youth club or another activity in which he will have had to try to be sociable, and ask him how it went. He needs to talk about why it was successful or not, so that he can understand how to improve next time.

This all takes time. Success breeds success, but the opposite is also true. You may need to be very specific with the instructions you give to begin with, in order for the child to be able to know what to do. This does make it harder for him to learn to adapt, but it may be the only route to success. He may need to see very clear steps to take before it becomes automatic.

SKILLS REQUIRED—FOR THE OLDER CHILD OR ADULT
This is directed at the individual who is learning these skills

Conversational

Meeting new people and keeping a conversation going. Decide who you want to meet, and have ready a topic to talk about, which you know he or she is interested in. Be careful where you stand or sit, and remember to give some eye contact, but not too much. If you can't think of something to say, ask a question. Try to smile, and don't just talk about your own problems. Others want to enjoy being with you, not to be exhausted by it. Try to stick to the topic under discussion. They will find it difficult if you jump from one subject to another.

Introducing others. Make sure you know their names and then wait for the right point to do this. If you don't know their names, ask them to introduce themselves. You could say, for example 'I know John from Cubs, and Fred from school, but I know you both like football.'

Waiting your turn. Remember what you want to say and then wait for the moment to say it. Look out for a pause in the conversation, make eye contact with the person who is speaking, and raise your hand slightly to indicate that you are going to say something.

Ending the conversation. You need to know how and when to end the conversation. You may need to leave to do something else, or the subject may have been exhausted. Wait for a moment when the other person has paused, and then use this as a point when you can say, for example, 'I have to go now to do . . .' Make sure you end the conversation in a friendly way: 'I have enjoyed this' or 'Can I give you a call?'

Social skills require you to be able to do the following:

- Understand when someone is teasing you, and how to respond.
- Share ideas and activities with someone else.
- Compromise when you don't get your own way and not show your anger.
- Say no when you feel uncomfortable about something you are asked to do. You need to have an idea of what is right and wrong.
- Be able to have and also express your viewpoint, and accept that other people may have a different one from yours.
- Say something nice to somebody else.
- Be able to accept a compliment from someone else.
- Ask for help when you don't understand and be able to say why you don't understand.
- Say thank you, which requires eye contact and the right tone in your voice.
- Keep a secret.

How do you show your emotions and strategies to cope?

- *Anger*. What do you do when you feel angry—shout, act it out physically? Do you have other ways of coping with it, and do you know why you have become angry? Count to ten, walk away, and think about what has happened and why. Think about ways you could get your anger out, such as exercise.
- *Failure*. Consider why you have failed. Ask someone close to you why as well. Have you thought what help you will require? Learn some relaxation techniques so that you can feel in control. Think of what has happened in isolation, it doesn't have to happen again. Move on.
- *Affection*. Tell the other person. Consider what you want to say, but make sure you choose an appropriate time.
- *Embarrassment*. We can all get embarrassed at some time and want to dig a hole and climb into it. No one else will remember five minutes after it has happened. Consider it over and move on
- *Feeling good*. Enjoy the feeling and reward yourself. You can do it, even if it takes a little practice.

TIPS FOR PARENTS

Activities to help your child's social skills

- ✓ Look out for pictures, stories in magazines, on the television—discuss them with your child. How would you feel in that situation, and how does it make him feel?

✓ Sit down together at a mealtime at least once a week and discuss what has happened to everyone. Go round the table and let everybody contribute, however young.

✓ What traditions do you have as a family? At Christmas time does one child always turn on the lights? Do you have a special meal on birthdays? Is Sunday night sloppy food night? Most of us have traditions. Talk about them with your child, and create some new ones. Let him create one—even if it is 'beans on toast night' on a Tuesday.

✓ Practise saying one nice thing about everyone in the family.

✓ Play a game of charades in which each person has to act out a feeling—for example, anxious, happy, sad—and then use this as an opportunity to talk about when and where you may feel like this.

✓ As a family or in a class, decide on a project, perhaps going on holiday. Divide up the tasks—where to go, where to stay, places of interest to see—and then make a time for everyone to feed back their information. Sharing activities like this makes it easier to make friends.

✓ Play a game together—a game of cards, or a board game —you then have to talk to one another. It also practises winning and losing

✓ Make your family shield—decide what should go on it. Each member could make their own and then discuss afterwards why they have chosen certain items to go on it.

✓ Talk about some of the 'harder' topics—sex, drugs, and relationships. Your child may have avoided these and he may need to understood what he feels.

✓ Read the newspaper headlines together, watch the news and discuss what he thinks about what is happening for that day.

✓ Ask your child about his day—the best bits, and the worst. With a younger child you could use a smiley chart, and let him choose which one he feels like. An older child could give a score out of ten, for example.

✓ Invite friends of yours home and let your child help you, passing round the biscuits or making them a cup of tea, for example.

12   Coping with Growing Up

All teenagers have to cope with growing up and seeing their bodies change. The teenager with co-ordination problems will now face enormous challenges with which he needs to cope. A growth spurt can also cause his co-ordination to deteriorate. Both girls and boys have different sets of problems that need to be considered. These may be mechanical, for example dealing with practical new tasks like shaving, and also emotional, such as dealing with making friends with the opposite sex. The ideas below are addressed to the young people for them to read, rather than to parents.

FEMALE HEALTH NEEDS

Make-up

Applying make-up is very important for many young girls, and will be a signal that they want others to see them as adults. If it is done badly it could be used as a point of ridicule.

The adolescent with DCD needs to be taught easy ways to make up. She may not instinctively see what suits her, what colours to choose and how to apply it effectively.

A make-up lesson is a useful way of doing this. She may listen more to an expert than to a parent.

Tips to help
✓   Techniques such as using a lip-brush or lip gloss may help. First make sure you are sitting down and are well balanced before even trying to put on make-up. If your balance is

poor then trying to do any fine motor task will also be
compromised.
✓   Too little make-up is always better than too much.
✓   Using a good magnifying mirror in a good light can make it
    simpler to see what to do.

✓   Putting on make-up in a regular sequence makes it into a
    routine and so easier to remember.
✓   Practising again and again when there is time and less pres-
    sure is the best way to gain the skills required—ask one of
    your friends or your mother what they think.
✓   Restrict the number of colours for eye shadow and lipstick.
    Try sticking to your skin tone and eye colour as opposed
    to the colour of clothes.
✓   Remember that it is also important to remove make-up
    thoroughly at the end of the day.
✓   Use large cotton wool pads—this makes the task easier than
    small ones.
✓   Some girls will try to pluck their eyebrows. If you have poor
    fine motor control this will be a difficult task. Let someone
    else shape them for you if you need to do so. It may be easier
    just to tidy them up. If you use mascara, think about having
    your eyelashes dyed. This only needs to be done a few times
    a year.

Hair

When leaving school and applying for courses or jobs, your
appearance is important and you will be judged on this, even if
you don't think it is important.

Tips to help
✓   A hairstyle that is easy to do and that stays neat is best.

Looking in a mirror can make it hard for you if you have perceptual and motor-planning problems—trying to sort out which is your left side and which is your right, for example.

✓   A style that can be almost 'rough' dried, that is dried with a towel, is best. It can then be finished off with a hot brush or some gel to keep it in place.

✓   Longer hair can be tied up with a 'scrunchie'. This is a covered bendy wire tie that just needs to be twisted to do up.

✓   Discuss with your hairdresser an easy-to-manage style. It is better to have something you can do yourself than to go for a fashion which is too hard to maintain.

Clothes

These need to be appropriate for the place and occasion. A girl going for her first interview needs to understand, for example, that high-heeled shoes and a short skirt may not be right! For individuals with co-ordination problems guidance may be needed as to what is actually appropriate.

Tips to help
✓   Placing clothes in order, either on a hanger or on the floor, makes it easier to colour-match. Look at them off before putting them on.

✓   If you are going to work in an office, you need to have appropriate office clothes—ask your boss what he thinks is right for the job.

Coping with periods

If stability, fine motor control, body awareness and sequencing are already problems, this will mean that when a girl starts to menstruate her difficulties may increase.

Tips to help
✓   It may be best to start by using stick-on pads (without side panels—or wings!). They don't require very good co-ordination.

✓   Using tampons may be too difficult. It does require some of the above skills. In school it may not always be possible to have the time or room to make sure that you are posturely stable to use them. If you want to learn, it may be best to try by starting to put the tampons in while sitting on the floor.

✓ You may need a reminder to change pads or tampons if you have poor time concepts and poor body awareness. A watch with a timer set to go off every few hours may be one solution to this.

Contraception

This may need to be considered for the older teenager or young adult who has or wants to become sexually active. Any form of contraception that needs to be taken on a regular basis may need a reminder to make sure that it hasn't been forgotten.

Tips to help

✓ As a young girl your choice has to be the partner using a condom, or the Pill or a depot preparation that you have as an injection every three months. The combined Pill contains both oestrogen and progesterone and needs to be taken within 12 hours of the same time each day. The mini-pill has only progesterone in it and needs to be taken at the same time each day.

✓ Using a buzzer reminder or a talking alarm clock will remind you that you need to take your pill each morning as you get up. If it is not part of a sequence of other activities like teeth-cleaning it may well be forgotten.

✓ Depot injections last for three months, so mean that you only need to turn up at the doctors or clinic then, and you could write this in your diary as a reminder.

✓ Remember that only condoms protect you from sexually transmitted diseases like AIDS and Herpes.

Some teenagers with these and other related problems may be more emotionally immature than their peer group, and may be seen as 'easy bait' for men. It may be necessary to be more protective for longer to ensure their safety. Reminders of appropriate behaviour and an understanding of why this is necessary should be kept simple to be successful. Video material, written material and tapes are available, targeted at this age group, which can facilitate a discussion.

Shaving, etc.

Tips to help
✓ Removing hair on legs or underarms may be difficult if you have poor fine motor co-ordination. Using a shaver with a blade that needs to be put on requires good dexterity. It may be better to consider using an electric shaver or a depilatory cream. Someone else applying a leg wax may also solve the problem.
✓ If you want to shave your legs it is better if this is done sitting down on the floor or on the edge of the bed, or sitting on the toilet seat. Standing in the shower feels unstable and could also lead to an accident.

Glasses and contact lenses

Tips to help
✓ The skill necessary to insert contact lenses, if you have poor fine motor co-ordination, may take some time and practice. A good light is important. It may be a new skill that could be learnt over a summer holiday when there is plenty of time, Psychologically, you will return to school with your 'new face' and this could well boost your self-esteem and confidence.
✓ If you wear glasses, make sure that they are not only comfortable but also suit your face. Going through adolescence is a time of great change and the need to think about appearance is important for your self-confidence.

Relationships

How do you cope with all the changes in emotions that are going on at the same time as school? You may have low self-worth after years of trying to cope with problems. You may have been bullied.

It is now time to be given the opportunity to develop your own interests and see yourself as a valued person. Friendships can help with this. You may well be a loner and have few friends. This can be a vicious circle—few friends means less practice at being sociable and less chance of improving.

✓ Consider joining an after-school club and evening classes, or doing some voluntary work so that you can meet other people who may have interests similar to yours, but no pre-conceived ideas about your difficulties.

✓ Try something new, you may find it leads you on to a job as well. Consider telling the leader or teacher where you may need some extra help when you start.

MALE HEALTH NEEDS

Colour co-ordination

As a teenager one of the key routes to success with your peers is appearance. How you look and sound are often a decider on who you will mix with. This often means 'blending in' with peers, such as wearing some key items that say you know what is in fashion or is 'cool' for now. This may also be locally related—for example, the local football team shirt, or wearing trousers or track pants of a certain style.

The adolescent with DCD may not have picked up on these clues and will therefore look different from his peers. If you are

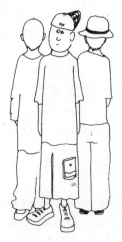

that person you may not think that this is important to you. You may feel that your *style* sets you out as an individual. For some people this is not a problem, but for others it will alienate them more, at a time when their social skills may be not be that good. If you are a parent, it may be up to you to talk about this if you feel it is affecting your child's relationships and to guide him through what he should be wearing. Sometimes an older sibling or friend can more effectively do this. Of course this does not mean telling him what he should wear each day, but discussing whether he feels he is making the friends he wants to, and how he could improve his success.

At a later stage, when interviews for jobs and college mean that a neater appearance is required, the boy may need to be taken through a checklist.

Tips to help
✓   Consider what will enhance your appearance and what suits you.
✓   Putting out clothes the night before on a hanger, so that they can be seen, helps to plan for this. It is easier to match colours off your person rather than on.
✓   Seeing that there are times to wear one style of clothes rather than another is an important message.
✓   Can you tie a tie? Would you be better choosing clothes with fewer fastenings, so that you can get dressed quickly?

Shaving

Once you need to shave on a regular basis, it is necessary to find a system that is easy, practical and safe. It is far better to use an electric shaver than a wet shave, as both blade insertion and shaving smoothly can be difficult. An electric shaver does provide a safety element and greater control.

Feet hygiene

Many adolescent boys are normally reluctant at this stage to keep their feet very clean. Some children with DCD do seem to sweat more and this affects their feet more than other areas.

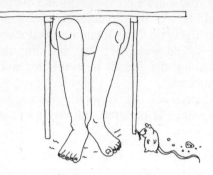

Tips to help

✓ It is important to wash between toes, dry properly and to make sure your toenails are cut straight across. This avoids getting in-grown toenails. A parent may need to do this for you, to make sure that it has been done satisfactorily and to ensure that the toes are clean.

Relationships

All children find growing up hard enough, but if you cannot grade your social responses then approaching the opposite sex may be even harder than usual.

How things can go wrong

Adam, a 16-year-old, went on holiday to the South of France with other children from his school. There were two other schools joining them. This was the first time he had been away, and he saw it as a great opportunity to meet other young people who would not know about his problems. He was attracted to one girl and they became friends within the first few days.

One evening towards the end of the holiday there was a disco, and he asked the girl to come outside with him for some fresh air. He reached towards her and tried to give her a kiss, grabbed too hard and pressed too hard on her lips. She screamed and called out and ran and told one of her friends. A teacher decided to act

on the incident and told Adam to stay in his room until it was all
sorted out.

After discussion with the teacher, it became clear that Adam
had no intention of hurting the girl and was very upset by the incident. It was his clumsy movements that had caused his actions,
and they had been completely misinterpreted. The other children
taunted him so much because of this one-off incident that he
ended up leaving the school and going to another local college.

Tips to help

✓ Learn about social distance. In a social group try to stand an
elbow's distance away from someone who is by your side
and an arm's length away from those who are in front of
you.

✓ Think about a topic you can talk about if the conversation
goes quiet. For example, a programme on television, a film
you have seen, a holiday you have been on, or somewhere
you would like to go.

✓ Don't go on and on, but let others talk as well. Listen to the
conversation and when they have moved on don't stick with
the subject you have just talked about. Practise this at home
and ask Mum or Dad to tell you when you have gone on for
too long.

✓ Find a hobby you like. If you are absorbed in this you will
be less likely to be worried about how well you are socialis-
ing.

✓ Give and take. You need to listen to others and to show that
you are doing so by nodding your head and responding to
what they are saying. Don't dominate the conversation. If
you are taking a girl out on a date, ask her what she wants to
do, and show her that you she is important to you.

LEARNING TO DRIVE *(see pp. 166–8)*

13 Adulthood and Gaining Independence

Many of the problems associated with DCD and dyspraxia when reaching adulthood are related to poor organisational skills and planning. The earlier problems of poor fine motor control may not have been overcome completely but can be avoided to some extent. As an adult you no longer have to wear a tie or have shoes with laces. You can also choose not to play rugby. You are in a better position to choose the things you enjoy and can accomplish and avoid those you have struggled with. Poor organisation makes it hard to try to gain independence and move on, and to enter the world of work or further education.

Some of the skills required are dependent on planning the path you wish to follow. This means obtaining good careers advice to guide you in the right direction.

Some of the strengths and difficulties for a person growing up with DCD

Strengths

- *Verbally able*. Verbal skills may be better than writing skills. You may have a good retentive memory, and seem to be able to store information from years before in great detail and to recall it with accuracy. Your short-term memory may not be as good, and information may need to be repeated before it becomes stored in your long-term memory.
- *Good computer skills* may have been developed because of

your need to bypass handwriting, and this may end up as an advantage to you.

- *Good creative abilities*—for example, photography, cookery or pottery.
- You may have become *very organised* to overcome problems and may find a structured environment suits you—for example, a small office or working with small numbers of people and with clear timeframes may be the ideal workplace setting.
- Many adults with DCD are very *understanding of the feelings of others*. They may be good with the young, elderly and with animals.

Weaknesses

- *Appearance.* At times a person with DCD may appear untidy. Recongnising the need to match the right colours or to wear appropriate clothes for a particular occasion may be skills that need to be taught rather than being learnt intuitively.
- *Organisation.* The problem areas may include appearing disorganised and finding it hard to budget at home, planning meals, or managing all the chores around the house.
- *Timing.* A sense and understanding of time may always have been a problem. As an adult, it is important to get up and get to work on time, as well as completing work set for you. It may be a skill that needs to be learnt.
- *Change.* This may produce feelings of discomfort and anxiety. Some adults say that they feel stressed when their timetable changes—for example, travelling or going on holiday may be stressful events. Adapting to any new environment may be stressful.
- *Signs of distractibility.* This may be something that you have had to try to deal with while growing up. You may have flitted from doing one thing to another without completing any one particular task. If this energy can be harnessed it can be used to good effect. Otherwise it may be hard to complete any work that has been started.
- *Visual perceptual problems.* Driving, for example, may be difficult. This affects judging both distance and depth. It means that skills like parking a car may be very hard to do.

Many cars end up with scratched wing mirrors and dents in the bumpers. (See pp. 166–8 for advice and tips.)

- *Bladder urgency.* The low-toned adult may always have had the problem of 'weak' bladder and this means there is little time allowed to get to the toilet, and the bladder may feel not fully emptied and require a second trip a few minutes later. There may be increased anxiety, for the individual, if there is no toilet nearby.
- Individuals with DCD *may tire more easily*. This is because both physical and mental efforts take more energy to achieve.
- *Manual and practical work.* It may be difficult to do DIY tasks in the house or handle cooking equipment in the kitchen—for example, using a tin-opener or slicing bread.
- *Emotional problems.* Some adults may be more likely to have problems with anxiety and may become depressed. They may have low self- esteem after years of not believing in themselves.

ADVICE FOR THE ADULT

Planning for college or leaving home

- Where will you live?
- First decide where you want to go, and what you want to do.
- Look at your strengths and weaknesses critically. Discuss them with others.
- Are you more of a loner, or do you like mixing with others of your age?
- How far do you want to be from home?

- Do you know other people in the area who could provide some support for you?
- Could you live alone, or would you be better off in a hall of residence where meals are provided for you, or in 'digs'?
- Would it be an option to go to college in your home town so that you could stay at home for a bit longer? Or could you move into a flat but near to your parents for some extra support?
- If you want to move to a flat, do you think you would be better in a bedsit, or could you share with others?
- Can you manage your finances over a week or longer?

If you want to go to college, have you considered the course?

- What type of course is it—a vocational one leading to a job, or would you need some further training afterwards?
- Would a practical course, working part of the time and having a day release at a local college, be better for you?
- If you decide on a practical course, are there procedures you would find difficult that you would then need to have help with to complete?
- A course where you are left to plan and organise your work on your own may be difficult. Consider that tight deadlines may be harder to achieve.
- Does the college or work placement have a special understanding and knowledge of adults with specific learning difficulties? Some are better than others.

Applying for the course

Let the course tutor know of your learning problems. If she is not told, there may be no extra dispensation given. It is much better to have a clear understanding of how to help from the start and to get the help that is available. Extra time may be required in exams and it is better to set this up as early as possible. You may need to have a report from an educational or health professional for extra provision to be given. The examiners will want to know how fast you can write. You may be able to have an amanuensis who would record the spoken words for you. If you are easily distracted it may even be necessary for you to be placed in a separate room to sit the exam.

Are you eligible for Disabled Living Allowance? Ask your GP.

You may also be eligible for grants for equipment, so if you have not been formally assessed it may be a step worth considering to get the extra help you may need. If you are a student you may be eligible for the Disabled Student's Allowance. This is a lump sum which can pay for equipment and services to help you.

The move to more independent living
At college or university you will need to plan your time out and budget for yourself. Set this up at the beginning of the term rather than run into problems later on. It may be better to set up a budget account to pay bills rather than wait for them to mount up.

Tips for good time management

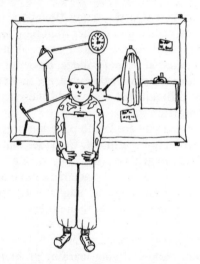

✓ *Time concepts.* Use strategies to remind yourself of the time.
✓ *Use a timer* in the kitchen, shower and at work, or a watch with a buzzer.
✓ *Use a notepad*, Psion, or organiser (Filofax) to remind you of what you need to do. Even a small notepad in your pocket is useful. There are electronic reminders you can buy on key rings.
✓ *Make plans* daily, weekly and monthly—don't wait until it all tumbles down on top of you and the deadline for work is tomorrow!
✓ *Reflect backwards* on 'mistakes' and how you could learn

from them—then move on (as they say, 'tomorrow is another day').

✓ *Organise* your day and week so you know what work you have to complete—have your checklist and tick it off as you go. You can then see how well you are doing.

✓ *Prioritise.* Consider what you need to get finished and what can wait. For example, you may be able to delay doing the decorating until after you have finished your exams! Decide what is important and has to be done, even if *you* don't want to do it.

✓ *Build in extra time.* We all think things will take us less time than they actually do. Allow extra time from the start, rather than running out and not being able to finish the task.

✓ *Try to be realistic* with your goals.

✓ *Prepare the night before.* There always seems to be more time then than in the morning, when you are trying to tear out of the door.

✓ *Get out* your clothes, map and papers, etc., in good time. Consider what you are going to have to do and where you are going, and go through it in your mind. You may then remember something else you require as well.

✓ *Keep two trays for mail*, and deal with it as it comes in. Place all incoming mail in the first and open it as it comes through, bills in the second and junk in the bin. Junk mail always seems to grow if it is left lying around, so if you don't want it, throw it out.

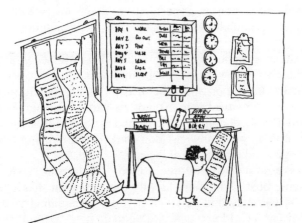

Below is an example of a weekly timetable that could be laminated so that it is reusable each week and put up on the wall to add to, and wipe off.

Weekly Timetable

MONDAY	TUESDAY	WEDNESDAY	THURSDAY	FRIDAY	SATURDAY	SUNDAY
Do English essay	Dentist		Pay phone bill	Go to tutorial	Pay the paper bill	
Take washing to launderette		Ring Mum and ask about holiday			haircut	
		Ring Alex about supper		Shop for weekend		
				Remember chocolates		

Dealing with feelings of isolation

Having co-ordination problems may have made it harder to make friends and improve on social skills. It may be even harder when starting at a new job or college to meet others, and may mean you feel very lonely.

Tips to help
✓ Join an evening or day class to learn or improve on a skill. This gives you an opportunity to meet others with similar interests and allows the conversation to be naturally focused on the area you are working on.
✓ Attend a support group for adults. You will see you are not the only one with the problems. You can share successes and gain support from the difficulties that others may also have had to overcome. You often learn some useful tips.
✓ Invite a work colleague home and make a simple meal, even if it is only a sandwich. You could prepare this in advance, or get a take-away meal instead.
✓ Take up a sport and join a club—all beginners are in the same boat. Adults are usually more tolerant than children, and you may find now that if you try something you found hard as a child you will be able to do it.

✓ Use the Internet as a means of gaining confidence and talking to others. When you get fed up you can just switch off. If you don't have a computer some libraries have access, and there are now cyber cafés springing up everywhere. Someone there will help you to get on-line.

✓ If you feel low all the time for more than a few weeks you may be depressed and should go and see your doctor. Depression can affect you in several ways and may make it harder for you to concentrate on the things that you enjoy. You may be finding that you are not sleeping so well at night. Perhaps you get off to sleep, but wake up in the early hours of the morning with everything on your mind. Your appetite may not be so good, and you may seem to eat because you have to, not because it tastes good. If you have a partner, you may have gone off sex as well.

Are you feeling guilty about how you feel, and thinking that other people are getting at you? Do you feel that nobody else understands how you are feeling? These are all signs that you may be depressed and require treatment. Treatment may be of the talking sort—called cognitive behavioural therapy. You may also require some drug treatment. Anti-depressants are not addictive and can help you to feel motivated again and able to achieve what you want.

AT HOME

Consider each of the following areas:

- Personal care
- Make-up (see tips on p. 143–4)
- In the kitchen
- Money management

Personal care

Tips to help

✓ Plan your wardrobe in advance—don't leave it to the last moment.

✓ Master and practise new fasteners and buttons while clothes are removed.

✓ Match your clothes with the event and your abilities.

✓ Practise tasks without looking—doing up zips and the top buttons on a shirt.

✓ Use easy-care fabrics and clothes without fastenings.

✓ Use alternatives to traditional fastenings—poppers and Velcro are easier to undo.

✓ Make sure you are balanced first when getting dressed. Consider sitting on the floor when dressing.

✓ Check which are the back and front of the garment—look for the label to remind you.

✓ For shaving, built-in safety guards and electric shavers are useful (see p. 149).

✓ Establish a routine so that tasks become automatic.

✓ Prepare in advance and avoid a rush—better to get up five minutes earlier and get to your destination on time, than to rush and feel sweaty and panic-stricken.

✓ Plan your drawers. Arrange things in the order you will put them on, and have a clothes-horse to hang them on. Make separators in the drawers so that everything doesn't just fall on top of one another, or use baskets to separate items out.

✓ Provide a seat for the shower so that you can sit down to shower if you have problems balancing.

✓ Place a bathmat in the shower to stop slipping.

In the kitchen

Tips to help

✓ Spend time planning meals—it will save you time when preparing for them. You can't make an omelette without eggs!

✓ Practise using different utensils at home when you have time.

✓ Check out handles of kitchen gadgets—there are some with rubber grips which are easier to hold.

✓ Start your own recipe book. Write out what you make, or just make notes of food you have had at other people's homes and ask them to write out the recipe. Tear out recipes you fancy in magazines. You don't need to stick to them exactly. Start with simple recipes and then adapt them. A pound of mince, onions and a tin of tomatoes can be turned quite easily into spaghetti Bolognese, cottage pie, chilli or lasagne, for example.

✓ Use convenience foods when entertaining if that helps.

✓ If you are in a rush, choose sandwiches or finger food.

✓ Organise cupboards and label drawers to make it easy to find everything.

✓ Know where water and electricity can be switched off.

✓ Sit if your balance is compromised.

✓ Use devices that make your life easier.

✓ The following items may be helpful in the kitchen:

> An electric can opener—this leaves your hands free
> A fixed board for slicing bread
> A separator for cracking an egg
> A rubber gripper or metal holder for opening a jar
> Bread spreader—this fixes the bread in one place while you spread it
> Tipper kettles to stop water spilling everywhere
> Plugs with handles—easier to pull in and out of the socket
> Sieve with rests—frees your hands to hold the spoon and the bowl
> A timer in the kitchen—when did you start and when are you finishing?

Use a menu planner to decide what you are going to make for the week, and what you will need to buy. You can look at this and see if you have made sure your meals are balanced nutritionally as well. This can also help with budgeting, making sure you have enough money to last the week. See the example below.

Monday	Chicken curry
Tuesday	Spaghetti with tomato sauce
Wednesday	Cheese and potato pie with baked beans
Thursday	Vegetable and bean casserole
Friday	Lamb chops and jacket potatoes
Saturday	Pizza and salad
Sunday	Roast chicken and potatoes and veg
Notes: Need to get- curry powder, pizza, more garlic	

Preparing a meal

✓ Plan the order of preparation and get out the necessary ingredients.
✓ Photocopy the page where the recipe is and tick it off as you go.
✓ Clear up as you go.
✓ Consider making a shopping list with two sides to it, one with the regular items you get every week and the other side with extras—see example below: You could have this laminated so that you could write on and wipe off the extra items each week. Or have some photocopied sheets that can be taken with you when you go out shopping.

Shopping list

REGULARS	EXTRAS
2 pints of milk	tomato purée
loaf of bread	garlic
margarine/butter	lamb chops
potatoes	deodorant
carrots	rice
onions	curry powder
yoghurt	chicken stock cubes
apples	tomato ketchup
cereal	
washing-up liquid	
loo rolls	
1 lb mince	
packet of chicken portions	
pasta	
tin of tomatoes	
1 lb cheese	
ham slices	

Money management

If you are going to live independently you need to consider how you will manage your money. It can be hard to have to think about what bills will come in at the end of the month, when you want to go out now and have a good time.

Tips to help
✓   Sit down with a pen and paper and write down all the bills you expect to receive—telephone, electricity, water, council tax, insurance, TV licence. If you have a car you also need to consider road tax, as well as MOT, petrol and servicing. Then put dates when you expect to have to pay them.
✓   Have you a bank account into which your earnings and any other payments are paid? If not, consider talking to the bank: there is usually someone there to help you set up a budget account. This allows a certain amount to be paid each month automatically and spread out over the year. It stops you running out of money when the bills come in. They will usually be happy to help you manage this.
✓   By planning weekly meals and budgeting for them, you can see how to make more economical meals and not blow all your money on pizzas and fish and chips, for example. Convenience foods can sometimes be quite a bit more expensive.
✓   Use your Citizen's Advice Bureau for local information about extra help available in your area. Fill in any forms at home, with help as necessary, when you are under less pressure.

PLANNING FOR THE WORLD OF WORK

You may have decided what you want to do. It's fine to be ambitious. You also need to be realistic about the steps you must take to get there.

✓   Look critically at what you need to do to reach your goal, and take small steps. Better to do it slowly and be successful than be unrealistic and fail.
✓   Start by taking courses that would lead to the final job you want. Think about what you would like to do and then

decide what steps are required to achieve it. You may need
to carry on in one job while at the same time retraining.
Sometimes this can take several years, but the end point may
be worthwhile. Some people today make several career
changes at different stages of their lives. This is no longer as
unusual as it was in the '70s and '80s.

✓ What could stop you? Is there something that makes it
harder for you because of co-ordination problems? You may
need to have some adaptations in equipment, or the
approach to learning may need to be different from that of
other students to help you achieve your goal. Are your
expectations really beyond your capabilities? Ask someone
who is close to you what they honestly think.

✓ How quickly do you want to get there? You may need to
consider doing some extra courses to lead you on to where
you want to go. If you left school without maths qualifications, you may need to go back to evening classes to get
them, but it shouldn't mean you can't do what you want.
There is often a way round it to achieve it.

How to choose your career

✓ *What are your strengths*? Liking a job and enjoying what
you do on a day-to-day basis is as important as anything else.
You need to know when you go to sleep every night that the
next day will be a good one for you, and that you are looking
forward to it. Consider your hobbies as potential jobs.

✓ *Verbal skills.* Are you good at talking to people or do you prefer to be on your own? If you can talk well but feel shy, are you better at dealing with people over the phone?

✓ *Organisational skills.* Are you totally disorganised so that you need to work in a very structured environment? Or have you overcome some of your problems and now have a good system and would be able help to organise others?

✓ *Are you* better one-to-one or in a group setting?

✓ *Caring for others.* Do you like working with the young or elderly, or with animals? Could you try out some voluntary work to see what it is like?

✓ *The Job Centre* has a careers adviser (Disability Employment Adviser) for individuals with learning difficulties, and they can place you in short-term positions to give you a chance to try them out.

✓ *The creative route.* Photography, writing, poetry—have you a hobby you could turn into a job? Do other people tell you that you are good at a particular thing?

✓ *Computing.* Are you good at computing because you have had to avoid writing? This could now be turned to an advantage.

✓ *Have you had work experience* in the areas you would like to consider? Try to do this: the ideas and the reality can be quite different. Consider your strengths and weaknesses, and decide the setting in which you would be most suited. For example, it is no good deciding you want to do hotel management if the first job you land is in a huge hotel. It may have hundreds of staff and you have to travel there in the middle of the night and find your way around the building. Much better, perhaps, to think of a smaller hotel with a friendlier atmosphere, near to home, and then move on when you have gained confidence.

Applying for a job or course

Remember the following:

✓ Your CV. Type it, and get someone else to write the covering letter if you think yours won't be neat enough.

✓ Practise the route to the interview—you don't want to be late.

✓ Practise interview skills with other people.

✓ Have some cards with you, showing your name and address—when you are nervous you may even forget your phone number!

✓ Get out your clothes several days before and ask for someone else's opinion about them.

✓ Tell your employer where your difficulties lie, but point out your strengths first.

✓ Have the correct money for the journey—you don't want to be worried about this when you are thinking about your interview.

LEARNING TO DRIVE A CAR

Are you having problems passing your written or practical parts of the test? There are books, videos and CD Roms available to help you with the written test, and you may be allowed extra time in the test on request. The problems that some individuals find when learning are as follows:

- Visual perceptual problems—the understanding of how far or near other objects are away from you. This makes parking difficult.
- Being able to see in wing mirrors and judging distances.
- Knocking the bumpers of the car.
- Integration—managing the gears, the mirror and the pedals all at once.
- Quickly being able to tell right from left.
- Going round roundabouts.

Tips to help

✓ It is probably better to consider learning with an automatic car. This decreases the number of things that have to be done at any one time.

✓ Some driving schools have simulated lessons where you can try out driving without setting out on the road until you feel confident enough.

✓ Request extra time for the written section of the test if you require it.

✓ Seek out an instructor who has taught individuals with disabilities—they may have more patience and have techniques that would help you.

✓ Mark the right side of the steering wheel with a red sticker

and the left with a blue one for a quick reminder.

✓ Plan your journey in advance. There are 'reverse maps' available, so you don't need to turn the map upside down on the way home!

✓ Map-reading—put a clip on the dashboard so that you can easily get to the map, but pull in to the side of the road if you are lost.

✓ Voice-operated systems for direction can help to take the problem away.

✓ There are cars that make a sound if you get too close to an object behind you.

✓ Remember to place a spare set of keys somewhere—but at the same time tell someone else where you have put them!

14 What Causes Dyspraxia and Development Co-ordination Disorder (DCD)?

To understand *why* dyspraxia and DCD occur and what then happens to the body it may be helpful to consider how the brain works and what parts of the nervous system fulfil different functions.

THE NERVOUS SYSTEM

The structure of the nervous system is made up of the two cerebral hemispheres, the cerebellum, the brain stem and the spinal cord.

The brain has two sides to it, called cerebral hemispheres, which are joined by a structure called the corpus callosum.

The nerves contain neurons, which are either sensory neurons, going from body to brain, or motor neurons, going from brain to body.

The muscles and organs in the body have receptors, which are there to react to changes in movement.

Sensory input allows us to be aware of our surroundings, to perceive changes and gain knowledge, so that we can plan our movements and co-ordinate our thoughts and emotions. We are able to process the information and we can then filter out unnecessary messages and process the complex instructions we have received, organise them and integrate them. The brain then decides on the message to the muscles and what movements are required.

The spinal cord

- It takes messages to and from the brain.
- It regulates functions of the internal organs.
- It does not integrate information, but rather passes it to and from the brain.

The brain stem

- This provides automatic activity, without the control of the brain—for example, respiration and digestion. If the brain is damaged breathing can still continue.

Vestibular nuclei and cerebellum

- The brain stem has nuclei that control and monitor gravity and movement in the inner part of the ear.
- The cerebellum is around the brain stem. This controls gravity, movement and muscle joint sensations; it makes the body carry out smooth movements and helps us to be able to balance.

Cerebral hemispheres

These are there for planning and performing an action in the body. There are several key areas:

- The limbic system controls emotional responses.
- The outer layer of the cortex. There are different areas for visual perception, speech and body movements.

There is an overlap between senses in some areas.

Lateralisation

This is the cross-over that occurs in the brain stem. Certain areas of each side of the brain control differing activities. If you are right dominant:

- *The left* hemisphere will control *fine motor tasks* and *language.*
- *The right* side will control *spatial relationships, visual and touch sensations.*

WHAT ARE THE UNDERLYING CAUSES OF DCD AND DYSPRAXIA?

First of all it has to be said that we are not entirely sure. It is very unlikely that there is only one cause, but several.

In the past children with dyspraxia and DCD were all thrown into one 'bucket' and were not examined in great detail for consistent similarities and differences. When this is actually done we then see that children do fall into different sub-groups under the umbrella of DCD.

DCD and dyspraxia as such are merely descriptions of the child's difficulties and indicate that these difficulties are motor-based—that is, the child has some co-ordination problems—but they don't say what has actually caused the problem.

Why do we not identify these problems from an early stage?

The child with severe physical or mental difficulties will usually be recognised as having problems as a newborn baby, either immediately after the birth or usually within the first few months of life. Today these may be picked up even earlier—when the baby is still in the womb. Problems are sometimes identified when the mother is scanned, and this is especially true if it is a physical problem that can actually be seen on the scan.

If the problem isn't picked up at this early stage then it is often noticed in the first few months of life, because of a delayed developmental 'milestone' such as sitting up, or a feeding problem like poor sucking or difficulty taking solids. Normally babies do certain things by a certain age. If they are later than the average then this means that the child is 'delayed'.

In contrast to the child with more severe learning difficulties, the child with co-ordination difficulties may tend to be noticed later. This may be at the stage when he starts to fail when compared with his peer group. It could be as late as around the age of seven, by which age one would expect him to have acquired certain skills and be more proficient in them and the gap between him and his peers is widening. Examples are getting himself dressed and being able to feed himself In addition, the child's handwriting should be at a legible stage and clear comparisons can then be seen.

The child with co-ordination problems may be referred to a paediatrician, to exclude certain treatable conditions or those which may have a genetic basis. There are some rare medical conditions, also affecting co-ordination, that the doctor would exclude; among them are the following:

Neurofibromatosis (NF1)
- This condition affects nerves and skin.
- It has a genetic basis.
- The signs of the disease are *café au lait* spots—brown patches on the skin—which may be quite pale in colour or darker. Some children have freckles in their armpits as well, or in the groin area. The neurofibromas that grow may be quite small or may grow to be firm or fleshy lumps under the skin.
- It can show itself as a child with low tone.
- NF can affect co-ordination and the child may have both fine and gross motor difficulties.

Benign congenital hypotonia
- This can show as a delay in motor milestones such as walking.
- The child may be low toned and be seen as a floppy baby.
- The child may show some delay in learning new skills.
- It often gets better as the child gets older.
- Gross motor skills such as catching and kicking a ball tend to be worse than fine motor skills such as handwriting.

Inherited connective tissue disease
- Affects skin, ligaments, tendons, joints, cartilage, bone, eyes, blood vessels and heart valves.
- Fourteen genes associated with this condition have been detected so far.
- It presents in varying degrees of severity.
- It can present as joint hypermobility. This means the joints are far more flexible than would normally be seen. There may also be delayed milestones such as walking. The child may appear clumsy and may have low muscle tone.

(It has been recognised that some DCD children do seem to be more mobile and 'bendy' and will sometimes have a parent with similar characteristics.)

Ehlers Danlos Syndrome Type (3) – Also known as Benign Joint Hypermobility Syndrome (BJHS)
- The child has increased joint laxity.
- Skin in some children is said to be very fragile and may bruise more easily.
- Joints may click.

Increased joint laxity
- Ten per cent of the population have increased joint laxity —this means they are more 'bendy' and flexible. The term commonly used is 'double-jointed'.
- It is more common in Afro-Caribbean, African, Indian and Chinese groupings.
- It can actually be beneficial to have increased joint laxity. Girls who have this can be very good dancers and gymnasts.
- Children and adults who have these types of problem often end up being seen in rheumatology clinics because of

aches and pains in their joints. The child and adult may compensate for their increased laxity by trying to gain some stability, but this may cause a strain on other joints. Sometimes, for example, the hamstrings will have shortened as a consequence of this. Some children dislocate their joints. Some children with BJHS have pain when handwriting and should be encouraged to use a computer if there is pain, especially to use a mouse rather than a keyboard.

SO WHERE DO THE PROBLEMS LIE?

Could DCD have a genetic basis?

Family patterns certainly exist in some DCD children where there are characteristics and problems that recur within the family.

Some children with problems who are seen have a mother or father who has clearly had similar difficulties as a child as well. We know that there are certain conditions like Ehrlos Danlos syndrome that have a genetic basis.

Could the problem be at a biochemical level?

In the rare disorder of galactosaemia, which is a biochemical disorder, children sometimes show co-ordination problems. There could be something going wrong at the level of the cells in the body that means certain 'messages' are not getting through as well as they should. At this time we are not clear where this is happening.

Is the problem at the level of muscle growth?

Muscular dystrophy is one condition in which the muscle fibres are abnormal.

Could the problem be caused during pregnancy?

Are the difficulties occurring because of an environmental 'insult'? This means something from outside us that causes the problems. The mother may not have had an adequate dietary intake of certain food substances or may have drunk too much alcohol, or she may have taken drugs illegally—or legally in the form of prescribed medication or smoking. These have not yet been identified. There is some debate at the moment that the problem may lie in the essential fatty acid metabolism, and this may have some relation to maternal diet in pregnancy.

DCD may well be due to a combination of these things. It is important to remember that the children we see are not uniform—each child has a different set of problems. There are, however, similarities that we can recognise between various groups. By building up this picture, we may then find that there are several types of DCD children and several causes of their problems. When we get to that stage, we shall be at the beginning of finding a potential cure.

Could the child develop problems as a consequence of illness?

Children with DCD may also have had glue ear. This may have affected their ability to acquire language skills at a crucial stage in their development. These children seem to have problems distinguishing sounds. They may shows signs of lack of concentration, may appear distractible, and may well be misdiagnosed as having attention deficit disorder. Glue ear is common but it seems to have a greater effect on those who have other problems as well, such as DCD and dyslexia. Is the child with DCD more susceptible to glue ear? This could be because some children are low toned and their posture means they don't drain their ears as well. We are awaiting more information.

Are some particular developmental delays of greater significance?

Some babies who have not crawled at all, or only bottom-shuffled, seem to be more likely to go on to develop co-ordination problems. Such a child will tend to sit on his bottom and not explore his environment. He can only see the world as far as 180 degrees. As far as he knows he doesn't have a back! He also cannot maintain his balance or turn round as well. The child consequently seems to have poor body awareness and little understanding that his body has a front and back.

The child who crawls moves all the way round his environment. He will crawl to an object and return back to his base. From this he will learn to understand distance—how far he needs to crawl to get the toy, for example. From this he can then learn the concepts of time. For example, if it takes three crawls there and back it will take XX amount of time to get there and back. These are skills that become ingrained at this stage in development, and if they are missed out at this crucial time will have a consequence for learning later on. We take for granted these skills that we naturally acquire and don't even think about them.

HOW DCD MAY BE CAUSED

The problem may occur at one level but then have an impact at other levels—the DCD cycle

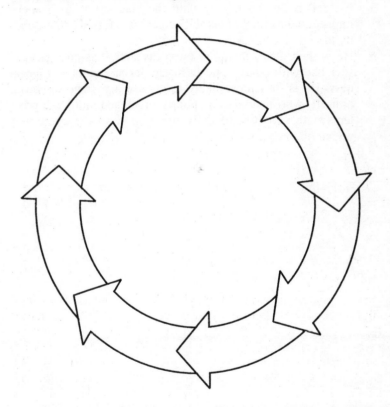

1   There could be an underlying predisposition to the problem. This means that you may carry the gene which makes you have increased laxity (or 'bendiness') and pass this on to your child.
2   The child may be born with increased laxity. His shoulders and hips are not as stable as normal and so he tends not to

crawl. This in turn gives him no opportunity to strengthen the muscles around his hip and shoulder joints.

3 The fact that the child did not crawl also seems to have a detrimental effect later on his understanding of time and direction, as well as more obviously resulting in poor gross motor function and body awareness.

4 The poor gross motor function and poor stability in the shoulders have an impact on fine motor function such as handwriting.

5 His failure to function well in the classroom has a social impact on the child, as his self-esteem is affected and his ability to organise himself.

6 He is then disorganised in everyday activities and tends to socialise with others who have similar strengths and weakness. He is thus more likely to choose a partner similar to himself, who may also be poorly organised and have problems with activities of daily living, and so the cycle may go on.

15 When Should DCD and Dyspraxia be Diagnosed?

One of the ways that health and educational professionals define DCD is to use the DSM1V criteria and ICD10 criteria. They are two ways of categorising DCD. They do not have a cut-off—that is, they do not give a statistical cut-off that can be applied to a population, saying that a certain percentage have the condition and another percentage have not. If they did this could be used for benchmarking if they were attached to particular tests that were also used as standard procedure.

Another problem is that one diagnostician (therapist or educational professional) will interpret the definition in a different way from another.

The term 'specific developmental disorder of Motor Function' is categorised by:

Specific Developmental Disorder of Motor Function (ICD10, World Health Organisation, 1992)
The child's motor co-ordination on fine or gross motor tasks should be significantly below the level expected on the basis of his or her age and general intelligence. This is best assessed on the basis of the individually administered, standardised test of fine and gross motor co-ordination. The difficulties should have been present since early development (i.e. they should not constitute an acquired deficit). (It is usual for the motor clumsiness to be associated with some degree of impaired performance on visuo-spatial cognitive tasks.)

The second definition is the DSM1V:

The DSM1V (American Psychiatric Association, 1994)
classification Chapter 3 Criterion A
Performance in daily activities that require motor co-ordination
substantially below that expected given the person's chronologi-
cal age and measured intelligence. This may be manifested
by marked delays in achieving motor milestones (e.g. walking,
crawling), sitting, dropping things, 'clumsiness', poor performance in sports and handwriting.
   Criterion B is that A significantly interferes with academic
achievement and activities of daily living.

What do we need to use to clarify the diagnosis?

● *Standard criteria used to define children with co-ordination
  difficulties*. What is currently used in a standard assessment
  may not include other elements that are closely associated
  with motor co-ordination difficulties, such as visual motor
  skills and auditory processing and vocal articulation and the
  level of social impairment. To fully understand the areas of
  difficulty, tests need to include all these elements.

● *A standardised set of tests used by both health and educational professionals to diagnose DCD*. If health and educational professionals used a common set of criteria, we would
  be able to see the true incidence of the condition.

● *An understanding by health and educational professionals
  of who should be eligible to give the diagnosis*. Should we
  be setting standards of training so that only appropriately
  trained persons can give the diagnosis? We then need to
  decide who those people should be.

● *The treatment used should be evaluated against improve-
  ments from a set baseline*. For example, if treatment X was
  given in these circumstances, we would be able to see what
  impact it had on motor co-ordination after a given time. We
  would all be measuring the same thing. This is like having
  lessons for your driving test, sitting it and then passing
  or failing according to your performance. It is a way of

measuring the improvement and also the skills of the person teaching you.

So how should we define children with co-ordination difficulties?

At the present time there is a lot of debate over the names given. This was a problem with dyslexia about ten years ago.

Dyspraxia is a term we have heard used more frequently over the past few years. It is one 'disorder' or specific learning difficulty within a spectrum of specific learning disorders, alongside dyslexia, attention deficit disorder and Asperger's syndrome. The term 'dyspraxia' is used by the lay public and by health and educational professionals as an umbrella word to signify a term meaning 'clumsiness'. It is also a 'label' now used by a wide range of health and educational professionals. Some of those have experience and training and some have just a little knowledge. This immediately causes some confusion as to whether a child really has the problem or not. So the whole debate about labelling begins. (See chapter 16 for more details.)

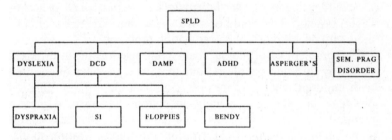

Why is a label important?

- Definition of what it is.
- Definition of what it is not.
- Counting the incidence in the population of a given condition.
- Planning for the population.
- Training the professionals.
- An action plan for the individual.

Dyspraxia

WHAT IS DCD AND WHAT IS DYSPRAXIA?

If an occupational therapist sees a child in a hospital children's centre setting, she will use the term dyspraxia in a very specific way. *She will use it to mean motor planning difficulties and perceptual problems.* However, if the child has co-ordination problems but is not dyspraxic under her specific criteria she will not use this term.

Should we be using *Developmental Co-ordination Disorder* (or DCD) instead? This could be used as *the* umbrella term for children with developmental co-ordination problems.

The problem of different labels being used to mean different things by different people is something that happens quite often with children who have dyspraxia and DCD. As co-ordination problems become more widely understood and there is greater recognition, there now seems to be more, rather than less confusion. There is a need for clarification and standardisation so that we all use the same language. Accurate assessment allows the treatment or help to be tailored to the problems of the individual rather than the label.

At the moment the debate on labelling which is occurring in the health and educational fields leaves parents with a sense of confusion. Some professionals are giving the diagnosis dyspraxia in a loose way, often using it to represent all 'clumsy' children rather than a specific group. The label when given by professional groups implies diagnostic skills with some degree of accuracy, but this is not always the case: the decision to apply it, and the standards and testing done, vary from profession to profession.

When is the label applied?

The educational and health decision about when the label is applied varies considerably from area to area in the UK, and indeed from country to country. Internationally it is often dependent on the provision of services and the financial implications this has upon them. If there are limited resources available, then rationing decisions will always have to be made. In some areas a child with co-ordination problems may not always be seen as high priority, especially when he or she is over 11 years of age. Most children's centres are overwhelmed with work and can only deal with the younger and the more disabled children, although because the DCD child has both living and learning difficulties it could be said that the impact on his life on a daily basis is as disabling as that of some children with a physical or mental disability.

The DCD child only becomes a priority when he is creating problems for other children, for example by having behavioural difficulties.

Compare this to other specific learning difficulties, such as dyslexia

Over the past 25 years there have been many areas in the UK where dyslexia didn't exist—it was not seen to be a problem. If you didn't look then of course you couldn't see. The views of some were that it was a middle-class problem, and provided a label for parents who didn't want to accept that their child was of low ability. Today things have radically changed in the area of dyslexia, although we now see similar problems arising in the recognition of the DCD child. Dyslexia now is not only recognised as a specific learning difficulty, but also as one that needs to be identified and the appropriate support given. This recognition is partly due to organisations like the British Dyslexia Association which provides resources, support and information for parents, and the Dyslexia Institute which has provided training for teachers and other professionals in addition to teaching for both children and adults. They have moved the boundaries for success for these children who 'didn't exist' until quite recently. Dyspraxia and DCD are certainly in the same position today as dyslexia was about ten years ago.

Do you know which label to apply in the first place?

The label that is applied depends partly on which professional the child finally sees. Can you imagine a doctor who has only three diagnoses that he knows? These, for example, could be migraine, appendicitis, and bunions. Anyone coming in to see him has to have one of those diagnoses. Then the treatment he knows is given accordingly.

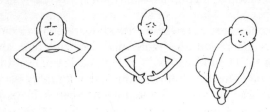

If you came in with a headache you could only end up with the migraine diagnosis; if you had abdominal pain it would be appendicitis, and if you had pain in your feet it must be bunions. Obviously this is an exaggerated example, but giving the label is dependent on training, current knowledge and experience. If you have never heard of dyspraxia you won't give that label, but you might give the diagnosis of dyslexia instead because there are similarities and it sounds roughly like the same sort of problem.

Fortunately we have moved on in medicine to widen our knowledge and understanding, but we are still at the early stages of fully comprehending the aetiology of children with co-ordination problems, and so mislabelling still occurs.

In the field of specific learning difficulties, for many years the only label an educational psychologist had in his box of tricks was dyslexia. Dyspraxia was not known about widely and would not have been taught as part of a training programme. Even now many training courses have little time spent on dyspraxia or DCD. This is also true for many of the health professionals, including GPs, who come in contact with children with co-ordination difficulties.

More recently, educational psychologists have been giving the diagnosis of dyspraxia. This may be arrived at by taking a history of the child's problems and then assessing him to see if his verbal skills are greater than his performance skills. How does this fit with the DSM1V and ICD10 criteria that we outlined on pp.

179–80, if we decide to use these as a way of saying whether a child has the problem or not? The tests used may not have looked at any of the activities of daily living at all, and may miss out on the social impact of the problem and the communication difficulties that may occur. However, the educational psychologist may indicate in his report that there are probably difficulties in these areas.

So how should we decide?

Is the educational psychologist in a position to make this diagnosis, or is this a health concern, or should it actually be a combination of both?

In an ideal situation both health and education should be involved in the diagnosis. There is a need to understand the child's intellectual function and his pattern of difficulty. We also

OT	PT	SALT	Behav Opt
Paedn	Neurologist	parent	child
Counsellor	teacher	clin psychologist	Educational psychologist
LSA/NNEB	GP	Ed. Authorities	HA

need to see if the child has global developmental delay or specific learning difficulties.

The ideal assessment

This would be an assessment that looks at the 'whole' child. Imagine if we examined the child just from the front and didn't ask him to turn round. We could miss completely that he had a lump on his back, for example. If we just tested his hearing, we would be unable to say whether he was blind as well. The DCD child does not usually have only one area of difficulty, so if we don't check the whole child we could miss a problem that has a crucial impact on the way that child can learn. The ideal would be as in the diagram on p.185, seeking information from all the sources. This is the ideal, of course. But we do need to consider all the facets, even if the child does not see all the specialists. We need to be asking the appropriate questions to highlight where the problems may lie.

Do children tend to have just one problem area?
Having one problem may make you more vulnerable to others. For example, if you have reading difficulties you may be more likely to have communication difficulties. Or is it the other way round?

Children with co-ordination problems may be more likely to have some psychological problems that then lead to poor motivation, concentration and difficulties with social interaction as a consequence, rather than a part, of the problem.

Which professional will make the diagnosis?

When occupational therapists, paediatricians or neurologists see children with co-ordination difficulties they may use the term dyspraxia, but this will usually only be applied after certain standardised and observational tests have been used and the child fits the criteria as having both motor planning and perceptual problems (see DSM1V criteria, p. 180).

The clinical psychologist seeing that same child may diagnose Asperger's, while the speech and language therapist may diagnose semantic pragmatic disorder. (see chapter 16).

Each of these groups has its own definition and criteria for diagnosis, but there is overlap in the problems that occur and functional and practical problems that exist with many of these children. There is certainly more overlap between the specific learning difficulties than has been thought in the past.

WHY LABELS ARE APPLIED

Legal reasons

There is more pressure on health and educational professionals to give a diagnosis than not to. This is because of cases that have been highlighted over the past few years. They have shown the consequences of failing to detect a child who has a problem and the consequences of that child not receiving the appropriate help.

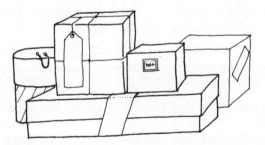

Educational reasons

What help does the child require? If he needs a statement of educational need, it helps to have a label attached. He is more likely to receive help.

Medical reasons

The label implies understanding and potential treatment. It helps us to define groups to look at the aetiology or cause of the problem and then to try to find a treatment for it.

Social and environmental reasons

Is there DCD or dyslexia in the jungle? Are we imposing labels because of the expectation for children at this end of the century? If one child in the family is bright, are the expectations for other children the same? Is there a need to seek out a label to give an explanation for a problem that has no diagnosis? The child may be of lower ability than his siblings, and this has to be accepted.

Research reasons

If we are to find solutions we need to define the population we are studying so that we can then count them and study them.

Parental pressure

Are we pressurised by parents to give a label? It is much harder to relate to other parents if you have not got a label. Parents would often prefer 'Itty-bitty syndrome' as a diagnosis than nothing. At least they could then join the support group allied to the problem, seek out information from books and the Internet and tell others what the problem was. They would no longer be seen as neurotic parents.

SHOULD WE CHANGE THE LABELS WE ARE USING?

The diagnosis of DCD is based on the *functional difficulties* of the child—the things the child cannot do. The name itself does not tell us about which 'bits' work well and which don't. The child with motor-based learning difficulties will have an overlap with other areas.

A different way of describing the areas of difficulty could be to use the following terms, and there may be others we could use as well: social, motor, speech and language, perceptual, reading and visual. These could then be graded as mild, moderate and severe.

This immediately gives the teacher in the classroom ideas of where the problems lie and which is the major problem area, which in turn helps professionals decide how to plan help for that child.

This method of using function as the descriptor seems more logical and relates to the practical needs of the individual child. Each one has a different set of strengths and weaknesses. As children are given help their function can be redefined and moved into the mild category rather than the moderate, for example. It even gives the child a chance to have the label removed altogether if he is functioning well, rather than being disabled with it. Is dyspraxia a diagnosis for life, or should we be looking at how well the individual is coping and attach help rather than labels to that person?

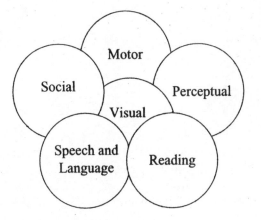

Should we remove labels altogether?

Parents ask if the child will grow out of the problem. There is no clear answer. The difficulties that we all face change at different stages of our lives. If the difficulty has gone, does that mean the child no longer has the disorder that was diagnosed? It is only worth holding on to it if the child or adult really benefits from this in some way. It may mean getting more help in terms of therapy or a payable allowance. It could mean meeting other people with similar experiences. Or it could actually prevent the individual from being fully accepted in the world of work: a potential employer might have preconceived ideas that would reduce the chances of the person getting the job. This could be because of previous experience of someone with dyspraxia who might have had very poor time-keeping and was disorganised. The employer now believes that all adults with dyspraxia have this problem. Perhaps it would be better to inform the employer of the person's strengths and weaknesses rather than use one umbrella term.

The problem of labelling is one that we are all faced with in all areas of disability, with no clear answers a lot of the time but many questions.

16 Differential Diagnosis

What else could the diagnosis be, if it is not DCD? How do the different conditions overlap? As discussed in the previous chapter, the diagnosis given is often dependent on the professional seen—in either the health or the educational sector—and on the problem presenting at the time, whether this is behaviour, co-ordination, reading, mathematics or language difficulties, for example. Some of the alternative diagnoses are merely a description of the child. They do not intimate the cause of the problem, whether this is genetic or environmental, for example. This is often because it is still unknown. By describing these other conditions, it is easier to see that there are overlaps between some of them and why confusion occurs. It also highlights how incorrect labelling may occur.

AUTISM AND ASPERGER'S SYNDROME

Autism is a disorder characterised by social impairments in important areas of development. These affect relationships, communication, understanding and imagination.

Autism is a 'spectrum' disorder, which means that in its most severe form it can co-exist with learning difficulties, extreme behaviour problems and avoidance of human contact. In contrast, there are people who demonstrate 'islets of ability', who may be severely handicapped in most areas but may display an extraordinary talent.

Asperger's syndrome

Children with a milder form of the disorder are often referred to as having Asperger's syndrome. They usually have average or above average intelligence and appear to shed many of the traits associated with autism as they get older. The social difficulties the child can have may be very subtle and mistakenly explained away in a multitude of different ways: maternal depression, marriage breakdown, poor parenting, even moving house. These reasons fail to address the intrinsic problem and it is important that parents should not feel that they have caused their child's difficulties.

Autism

Children with autism go through various phases. From two to five years of age behaviour is often very difficult and the autistic pattern is seen in its most typical form. Some improvement in sociability, skills and behaviour can be expected from six to twelve years. During the teens and twenties problems may reappear or become more marked. These are linked to the need to be independently sociable. Difficulties tend to lessen again in later life when choices about how you conduct yourself become greater.

The following are some features of autism:
1 Gross and sustained impairment of emotional relationship with people. They do not mix well with others.
2 Self-examination.
3 Preoccupation with particular objects, or certain characteristics of them, without regard to their accepted functions, persisting long after the baby stage—for example, spinning wheels, fascination with lines and so on.
4 Sustained resistance to change in the environment and a striving to maintain order or sameness—they can become very distressed because of change.
5 Behaviour leading to suspicion of abnormalities of the special senses in the absence of any obvious physical cause—for example, the child is not responsive to sound but has no hearing loss; cannot tolerate certain sounds; looks at objects from the corners of his eyes.
6 Abnormalities of mood. The child's mood can vary, and this may be difficult to predict.

7   Speech disturbances.
8   Disturbance of movement and general activity, such as run-
    ning around without any particular purpose evident, some-
    times toe-walking or flapping the hands.
9   A background of serious retardation in which islets of normal,
    near normal, or exceptional intellectual function or skills may
    appear. At times the child can behave like other children.

PRAGMATIC LANGUAGE DIFFICULTIES

Semantic means the meaning of words and pragmatics is the
social use of language. This is seen in the non-autistic child who
has problems in conversational relevance—that is, understanding
the meanings of words not just in isolation but in the context in
which they are used. For example, 'The sky is *deep* blue
today—what does *deep* mean in this context?

*James was a child with these problems. On one occasion he was
told by his teacher, 'That was excellent work, you got 9 out of 10
for that, one wrong.' For the rest of the term James tried to get 9
out of 10 because he had understood that that was what she
wanted him to do!*

Semantic pragmatic disorder can affect reading, verbal and non-
verbal cues, as well as social functioning. The child may sometimes give out too much or too little information, butt into a
conversation too soon, and may not be good at turn-taking. He
may not seem to understand what is being asked of him. The term
is generally used and given by speech and language therapists.

The child with these problems may read well but not understand the context of what he is reading. He may seem to have flu-
ent language and be able to hold a conversation, but on closer
examination one can see he does not understand some of the concepts of language. He may not understand time and space and
sometimes has difficulty with the parts of language that give
meaning, like 'on', 'under', 'through', 'over', 'now' and 'later'.
He may not see obvious groupings and similarities between
objects that other children will see—for example, that a potato,
cucumber and cabbage are all vegetables.

Such a child tends to see things very literally—if you said
to him, 'Pull up your socks', he would do exactly that and not

see the other, less literal, meaning. Starting and stopping conversations is difficult for him. His understanding of his social circumstances may be poor.

Many of these problems are similar to those of the child with DCD—social understanding, concepts of time and distance, for instance.

ADHD (ATTENTION DEFICIT HYPERACTIVITY DISORDER)

ADHD has been recognised since the days of Ancient Greece, and the core symptoms are overactivity, impulsivity, and distractibility. Approximately one in twenty children are thought to have ADHD. Males are diagnosed three to seven times more often than females.

ADHD is not a disorder that can be identified by one test. It is usually diagnosed by observation. It depends how often the child behaves in this way, how bad the problem is and how long it has been going on. Before this diagnosis can be made the symptoms have to have been present from a young age, and the child should have the problems in most settings. This is why it is important for both the parent and the doctor to make sure that there is a clear picture of how the child behaves both at school and at home. It is true that in different circumstances individuals will appear better or worse—trying to keep quiet in church is different from watching a football game. It also depends what is expected from you. Children with ADHD can show variable patterns of behaviour.

Over 50 per cent of individuals diagnosed with ADHD also

meet the criteria for at least one other psychiatric or learning disorder. Children can present with behaviour that may be misdiagnosed as ADHD when the cause is actually, for example, dyspraxia, hearing problems, Tourette's syndrome, trauma including abuse, speech and language difficulties, dyslexia or Asperger's syndrome. It can, however, occur in conjunction with some of these problems.

ADHD is not about poor parenting or poor teachers. Parents are often at their wits' end trying to cope with a child whose behaviour impacts on the whole family. They believe that it must have been caused by something that has happened in the family, such as a divorce, or by spoiling the child too much at a younger age. Help for parents needs to be practical and provide strategies to help them on a daily basis. Support for the parent is paramount, as other people's attitude to them and their child may compound the problems. It often feels very embarrassing for a parent trying to explain their child's behaviour. Other people are sometimes quick to judge the parent and make the decision that it is they who are the problem.

What should you do if your child as been given a diagnosis of ADHD as well as dyspraxia?

Tips to help

✓ Understand the problem and consider how your child feels; this will allow you not to blame yourself or your child.
✓ Boundary setting—try to explain the consequences of his actions, but be patient.
✓ Provide boundaries for the child in a consistent way—your behaviour needs to be consistent even if his is not always so.
✓ Don't delay feedback.
✓ Reward your child for good behaviour, rather than reprimanding him when he misbehaves—he will expect you to tell him off. Reward can be a treat or simple praise.
✓ Using a token system can help some children.
✓ Consider drug treatment in some children if behaviour modification has failed. Ritalin (methylphenidate) is the most commonly used drug treatment. It is started at a lower dose and gradually increased up to a twice-daily dose. It is usually given after breakfast and after lunch, and its effects last

about four hours. Some children need a further dose at four o'clock. Some children may be sensitive to it and find their appetite decreases, or it may disturb their sleep pattern, but if the dose is adjusted this may be controlled.

Dexamphetamine and Imipramine are two other drugs that may be used. All of them have to be prescribed under specialist supervision.

Under six years of age the incidence of side-effects is greater, so this needs to be considered before starting treatment.

What problems does the child with ADHD have in the classroom?

- *Talking out of turn.* These may be unsolicited words to the teacher or other class members, not always in line with the activities taking place in the classroom. This is called impulsivity. Impulsivity can also lead to dangerous behaviour, such as running out into a road without looking at all.
- *Out of the seat.* When the class has been told to be seated the child cannot remain seated and seems fidgety.

ADHD may be misdiagnosed from the above behaviour, as the child with DCD may also appear distractible and fidgety. This may be because he may not be able to filter out sounds and movements easily in the classroom. He may also feel posturally unstable (wobbly) in his seat. By correcting some of these elements, the fidgety behaviour may be reduced considerably.

DAMP

This is Deficit in Attention, Motor Control and Perception, and is a term used more in Scandinavian countries than in the UK. It is a combination of DCD and ADHD. There seems to be some evidence for a link with maternal smoking in this group. If the child has difficulties in co-ordination and distractibility, it seems to have a greater impact on learning in the classroom—not surprisingly, as it makes it harder for the child to learn in this situation.

DYSLEXIA

This is a combination of abilities and difficulties which affect the learning processes in one or more areas of reading, spelling and writing. There may be associated difficulties in areas of short-term memory, auditory sequencing and visual perception, spoken language and motor skills. Some children show good creative and/or oral skills. The child may have problems with sequencing activities. He can have good and bad days. He may also show a difference in directional words such as 'up' and 'down', 'in' and 'out'.

At primary school age the child may write letters and figures the wrong way round. He may have difficulty remembering tables and the alphabet. He may also confuse 'b' and 'd' and other letters. He may not be able to understand what he has read. The older child may have problems planning and organising his work. He may confuse times and dates. He may also need to have instructions repeated over and over again. The child may still read inaccurately and have difficulties with spelling.

DYSCALCULIA

This means a difficulty with mathematical concepts and learning. It may affect a number of areas:

Linguistic skills—that is, those needed to understand mathematical terms, understand the symbols and be able to decode written problems into mathematical symbols.
Perceptual skills—recognising or reading numerical symbols or arithmetical signs and being able to put objects into groups.
Attention skills—copying numbers or figures correctly and being able to remember the signs being used (add, divide and so on).
Mathematical skills—following a sequence of mathematical steps, counting objects and learning mathematical tables.

Tips to help
✓ Work on language concepts so that the child understands 'in', 'on', 'over', 'top', 'bottom' and so on in the world around him before transferring this into mathematical problems for him.
✓ Sequencing activities will help the child. Use everyday

examples such as which pan in the kitchen is first off the shelf, which second, and so on. Get your child to tell you which are the biggest and smallest bowls in the cupboard.

✓ Does your child understand which order numbers come in—that 1 comes before 2 and so on? Get some magnetic numbers and use them for this on the fridge door.

✓ Make a feely bag and get the child to guess which numbers are which before removing them from the bag.

Glossary of Terms

Apraxia: the lack of praxis or motor planning. Interference with planning and executing an unfamiliar task.

Articulation: the production of vowels and consonants by the active and passive articulators in the mouth. The active articulators are the moving parts of the mouth (lips/tongue/soft palate) which can produce sounds, whilst the passive articulators are the non-moving parts of the mouth (hard palate, teeth) against which, in the production of many sounds, the active articulators come into contact.

Asymmetry: one side of the body is different from the other.

Auditory: pertaining to hearing.

Auditory discrimination: the ability to recognise differences in phoneme. This includes the ability to identify words and sounds that are similar and those that are different.

Auditory perceptual problems: difficulty in taking information through the sense of hearing and/or processing that information. The child may hear inaccurately.

Auditory sequential memory: the ability to hear a sequence of sounds or words or sentences and be able to hold them in the memory for sufficient time to be able to gain information from them, process that information and respond to it.

Balance: ability to stay in and regain a position such as standing and sitting.

Beery: a development test of visual motor integration.

Bilateral: refers to the ability to co-ordinate both sides of the body.

Bilateral integration: the ability to move both sides of the body in opposing patterns of movement, such as jumping sideways.

Body awareness: the sensory knowledge of oneself moving through space.

Body image: the visual knowledge of oneself.

Body percept: a person's perception of his own body, consisting of sensory pictures or 'maps' of the body stored in the brain. It may also be called the body scheme or body image.

Body scheme: the sensory knowledge of onseself.

Central programming: neural functions that are innate within the central nervous system; they do not have to be learned. Crawling on hands and knees and walking are good examples of centrally programmed actions.

Cerebral palsy: permanent, but not unchanging, disorder of posture and movement resulting from brain damage.

Cluttering: rapid and muddled speech.

Co-contraction: the simultaneous contraction of all the muscles around the joint to stabilise it.

Co-ordination: muscles working together to achieve smooth, efficient movements.

Development: process of growth of all body parts and functions, physical, emotional and intellectual.

Directional awareness: the ability to move in different directions such as forwards, backwards, and sideways.

Distractible: not able to concentrate.

Dominance: relates to the side the child uses to carry out activities that require just one side to be used, such as writing, kicking a ball, looking through a tube.

Dysarthria: the articulation of language leading to slurred speech.

Dyscalculia: a problem with mathematical concepts.

Dysgraphia: extremely poor handwriting or the inability to perform the motor movements required for handwriting.

Dyslexia: difficulty in reading or learning to read.

Dyspraxia: poor praxis or motor planning, a less severe but more common dysfunction than apraxia.

Equilibrium: refers to body movements or shift in weight in order to regain/maintain balance.

Expressive language: communication by means of the spoken word. The ability to produce spoken language that is grammatically and syntactically sound and coherent in both content and sequence.

Extension: the action of straightening back, neck, arms or legs.

Eye-hand co-ordination: the ability of the eyes and hands to work together. It is needed for writing, for example.

Fine motor: see p. 27.

Finger agnosia: the ability to recognise which finger is being touched when vision is excluded.

Flexion: the act of bending or pulling in a part of the body.

Floppy: parts (or all) of the body that feel very loose and can be moved in a greater range than you would expect.

Grapheme: individual letters of the alphabet.

Gross motor see p. 28.

Higher level language: the ability to process, integrate, interpret and organise verbal and written language.

IEP: individual education plan for the child with special educational needs.

Kinaesthesia: the knowledge of where your body is in space.

Midline: this develops out of laterality. A child needs to have a well-defined midline in order to develop a sense of space around him and be able to orientate himself and his surroundings.

Midline crossing: the ability to cross one hand from one side of the body to the other, required for activities such as handwriting.

Minimal brain dysfunction: a mild or minimal neurological abnormality that causes learning difficulties in the child with near-average intelligence.

Minimal crossing: the ability of your hand to cross from one side of the body to the other.

Motivation: a desire to do something.

Motor planning: the ability of the brain to conceive and organise and carry out a sequence of unfamiliar actions—also known as praxis.

Occupational therapy: management of activities of daily living and educational skills.

Optometrist: tests people's vision and prescribes glasses.

Oral peripheral examination: the passive and active oral structures are investigated to ascertain the existence of any abnormality. Their function is then determined to ascertain whether any breakdown in the accuracy/speed/sequencing co-ordination of movement could be contributing to decreased speech intelligibility and exacerbating feeding patterns.

Orthoptist: a paramedic who specialises in the movement of the eyes and children's visual problems.

Pelvic stability: relates to the joint laxity and the muscle strength of and around the hips.

Perception: the meaning that the brain gives to sensory input. Sensations are objective, perception is subjective.

Perceptual constancy: the ability to perceive an object as possessing certain properties such as shape, position and size in spite of the different ways it may be presented.

Phoneme: speech sound.

Phonological awareness: the understanding that language is made up of individual sounds which are put together to form the words we write and speak. It is the ability to identify numbers of syllables and repeat multisyllabic words to detect or generate rhymes, to blend and segment words into their component syllables and sounds. These skills are important prerequisites for developing reading, writing and spelling.

Physiotherapy: management of the movement disorders.

Posture: a position from which a child starts moving, any movement when it stops.

Pragmatics: the social use of language.

Prone: the body position with the face and stomach downward.

Propioception: from the Latin word 'one's own'. The sensations from the muscles and joints. Propioceptive input tells the brain when and how the joints are bending, extending or being pulled or compressed. This information enables the brain to know where each part of the body is and how it is moving.

Receptive language: the ability to understand language.

Reflexes: always exactly the same response to certain stimuli —for example, turning the head to the left causes extension of the limbs on that side, and flexion of limbs on the other side.

Refractive error: the lens power required to produce a perfectly focused image on the retina.

Semantic: the meaning of words.

Sensory input: the stream of electrical impulses flowing from the sense receptors in the body to the spinal cord in the brain.

Sensory integration (SI): a process that describes the ability to organise sensory information for use.

Sequencing: the ability to master individual steps and activities and pass from one component part to the next in the correct order.

Shoulder stability: relates to the muscle strength and joint laxity of the shoulders.

Skill: the efficiency of carrying out a task.

Spatial awareness: the ability of the child to judge distances and direction of himself in relation to other objects.

Spatial orientation: knowledge of space and the distance between the self and objects in the environment.

Speech and language therapy: management of eating, drinking, speech and language and communication difficulties.

Stereognosis: the ability to perceive and understand the shape and size and texture of objects by the sense of touch alone.

Supine: horizontal position with face and stomach upward.

Symmetrical integration: the ability to move both sides of the body simultaneously in identical patterns of movement. A child should be able to jump forwards with both feet together 10 out of 10 times.

Tactile defensiveness: a sensory integrative dysfunction in which tactile sensations cause excessive emotional reactions, hyperactivity or other behavioural problems.

Tone: firmness of the muscles.

TVPS: a non motor test for visual perception.

Vestibular system: the sensory input that responds to the position of the head in relation to gravity and decelerated or accelerated movement.

Visual: pertaining to sight.

Visual closure: the ability to recognise an object when presented as an incomplete form.

Visual discrimination: the ability to discriminate similarities and differences in characteristics, arrangements, sequences or organisation of visual stimuli.

Visual figure ground: the ability to differentiate stimulus from its background or the ability to attend to one stimulus without being distracted by irrelevant visual stimulus.

Visual memory: the ability to recall characteristics of stimuli through vision only.

Visual motor integration: the integration of visual motor information which enables eye-hand co-ordination, that is required to carry out activities.

Visual perception: judging depth, visual closure, visual discrimination and visual figure ground—that is, difficulty processing information, seeing the difference between two objects, trouble seeing how far and near objects might be.

Visual spatial relationships: the ability to sense the relationship of objects with each other and yourself. Depth, length, position, direction and movement are all aspects of this sense.

Word finding difficulties: one has difficulty thinking of the word one wants to say quickly and accurately, even though one does know the word. These difficulties interrupt attempts at conversation and are frustrating for the speaker as well as the listener.

Directory of Resources

This is not a definitive list and is a starting point for your exploration regarding more information for your child or school. It will help you to know where to go for further help or information.

This should not be seen in any way as an endorsement or recommendation of these organisations.

CHILDREN

Bullying

Anti-Bullying Campaign
185 Tower Bridge Road, London SE1 2UF
Tel: 020 7378 1446. Fax: 020 7378 8374
Mon-Fri, 10 am – 4 pm

Kidscape
2 Grosvenor Gardens, London SW1W 0DH
Helpline: 020 7730 3300. Fax: 020 7730 7081
E-mail: webinfo@kidscape.org.uk
Website: www.kidscape.org.uk

PARENT SUPPORT ORGANISATIONS

Independent, governmental and charitable bodies

The Children's Legal Centre
University of Essex, Wivenhoe Park, Colchester,
Essex CO4 3SQ.
Tel: 0845 120 3747
Website: www.childrenslegalcentre.com
*An independent national body concerned with the laws and
policies which affect children and young people in England and
Wales. It provides free advice and information by phone.*

DfES
Sanctuary Buildings, Great Smith Street, London SW1P 3BT.
Tel: 020 7925 5000
E-mail: info@dfes.qsi.gov.uk
Website: www.parents.gov.uk

The Dyscovery Centre
4A Church Road, Whitchurch, Cardiff CF14 2DZ
Tel: 029 2062 8222
E-mail: dyscoverycentre@btclick.com
Website: www.dyscovery.co.uk
*Provides an interdisciplinary team of health and educational
professionals. The centre assesses and treats children and adults
with living and learning difficulties including Dyspraxia.
It also provides resources, equipment and toys.*

Association of Educational Psychologists
26 The Avenue, Durham, DH1 4ED
Tel: 0191 384 9512. Fax: 0191 386 5287
Website: www.aep.org.uk
Will supply details of psychologists in particular areas.

Advisory Centre for Education (ACE)
Department A, Unit 1c, 22-24 Highbury Grove, London
N5 2DQ
Tel: 020 7354 8321. Fax: 020 7354 9069
Helpline: 0808 800 5793
E-mail: ace-ed@easynet.co.uk
Website: www.ace-ed.org.uk
Publishes guides for parents on the education system.

Advisory Unit: Computers in Education
126 Great North Road, Hatfield, Herts AL9 5JZ
Tel: 01707 266 714. Fax: 01707 273 684
E-mail: sales@advisory-unit.org.uk
Website: www.advisory-unit.org.uk
*Offers advice and training, information and technical support
in the use of IT to support pupils with learning difficulties.*

Centre for Studies on Inclusive Education (CSIE)
Room 2S 203, S Block Frenchay Campus, Coldharbour Lane,
Bristol BS16 1QU
Tel: 0117 328 4007. Fax: 0117 328 4005
Website: www.inclusion.org.uk/csie
*A charity committed to working towards an end to all forms of
segregated education.*

Education Otherwise
P. O. Box 7420, London N9 9SG
Tel: (Helpline) 0870 730 0074
E-mail: enquiries@education-otherwise.org
Website: www.education-otherwise.org
*Self-help organisation offering support, advice and information
to families contemplating home-based education.*

Parentline Plus
Control Office, Unit 520, Highgate Studios,
53–57 Highgate Road, London NW5 1TL.
Freephone: 0808 800 2222. Fax: 020 7284 5501
E-mail: parentsupport@parentlineplus.org.uk
Website: www.parentlineplus.org.uk

The Nuffield Centre Dyspraxia Programme
Nuffield Hearing and Speech Centre, RNTNE Division
of Royal Free, Hampstead NHS Trust, Grays Inn Road,
London WC1X 8DA
Tel: 020 7915 1535

Network 81
1-7 Woodfield Terrace, Stansted, Essex CM24 8AJ
Tel: 01279 647 415, Mon-Fri 10 am – 2 pm
Fax: 01279 814 908
E-mail: network81@btconnect.com
Website: www.network81.org
National network of parents of children with special educational
needs. Working towards properly resourced inclusive education.

Pre-School Learning Alliance
69 Kings Cross Road, London, WC1X 9LL
Tel: 020 7833 0991 Open Mon-Fri, 9 am – 5 pm
Fax: 020 7837 4942
E-mail: pla@pre-school.org.uk
Website: www.pre-school.org.uk
National telephone helpline for parents seeking help and
guidance in finding suitable childcare.

Parents at Work
45 Beech Street, London EC2Y 8AD
Tel: 020 7253 7243
E-mail: office@workingfamilies.org.uk
Website: www.parentsatwork.org.uk
Campaign to support working parents of children with
disabilities and special needs.

IPSEA
(Independent Panel for Special Education Advice)
6 Carlow Mews, Woodbridge, Suffolk IP12 1DH
Tel: 01394 381 518. Helpline: 0800 018 4016
Website: www.ipsea.org.uk
Helps to guide parents through the assessment and tribunal
processes. They can represent parents at tribunals.

CreSTed (Council for the registration of Schools teaching
Dyslexic pupils)
Greygarth, Littleworth, Winchcombe, Cheltenham GL54 5BT
Tel: 01242 604 852. Fax: 01242 604 852
E-mail: admin@crested.org.uk
Website: www.crested.org.uk
List of schools who specialise in helping pupils with Dyslexia
and some who help children with Dyspraxia.

Parents for Inclusion
Unit 2, 70 South Lambeth Road, London SW8 1RL
Tel: 020 7735 7735. Helpline: 0800 652 3142, 10am–3pm
Website: www.parentsforinclusion.org
Works to encourage people with disabilities to have a normal
life in the community on an equal level with others without
physical and social barriers.

Contact-a-Family
209-211 City Road, London EC1V 1JN
Tel: 020 7608 8700. Fax: 020 7608 8701
Helpline: 0808 808 3555
E-mail: info@cacamily.org.uk
Website: www.cafamily.org.uk
Gives support for families who care for children with disabilities
who have special needs.

SPECIAL NEEDS CHARITIES

Dyspraxia Foundation
8 West Alley, Hitchin, Herts SG5 1EG
Tel: 01462 454 986. Fax: 01462 455 052
E-mail: admin@dyspraxiafoundation.org.uk
Website: www.dyspraxiafoundation.org.uk
*Provides support and resource material and has groups for
parents and separate groups for adults across the UK.*

Ehlers Danlos Support Group
P.O. Box 337, Aldershot, Hampshire GU12 6WZ
Tel: 01252 690 940
Website: www.ehlersdanlos.org

I-CAN
4 Dyer's Building, Holborn, London EC1N 2QP
Tel: 0870 010 4066
E-mail: ican@ican.org.uk
*Specialises in the education of speech and language impaired
children.*

The National Autistic Society
393 City Road, Stratford, London EC1V 1NG
Tel: 020 7833 2299
E-mail: nas@nas.org.uk
Website: www.nas.org.uk
*Runs an advisory and information service for people with autism
and related disorders such as Asperger's syndrome.*

AFASIC (Association for speech impaired children)
69-85 Old Street, London EC1V 9HX
Tel: 020 7841 8900. Fax: 020 7841 8901
Helpline: 0845 355 5577
E-mail: info@afasic.org.uk
Website: www.afasic.org.uk

The British Dyslexia Association
98 London Road, Reading RG1 5AU
Tel: 0118 966 2677. Fax: 0118 935 1927
Helpline: 0118 966 8271 (Open 10 am–12.30 pm/2–4.30 pm,
Mon-Thurs)
E-mail: admin@BDAdyslexia.org.uk
Website: www.bda-dyslexia.org.uk
*A national organisation for people with specific learning
difficulties. It provides support, advice and information on
dyslexia.*

The Scottish Dyslexia Association
Unit 10, Stirling Business Centre, Wellgreen, Stirling FK8 2DZ
Tel: 01786 446 650. Fax: 01786 471 235
Helpline: 0844 800 8484
E-mail: info@dyslexiascotland.org.uk
Website: www.dyslexiascotland.org.uk
*A national voluntary organisation aiming to raise public
awareness of dyslexia and its related difficulties.*

Scope
6 Market Road, London N7 9PW
Tel: 020 7619 7100. Helpline: 0808 800 3333
E-mail: cphelpline@scope.org.uk
Website: www.scope.org.uk
*Supports people with cerebral palsy and their parents and
carers.*

The Hypermobility Syndrome Association (HMSA)
12 Greenacres, Hadleigh, Benfleet, Essex SS7 2JB
Tel: 0845 345 665
Website: www.hypermobility.org
*Aims to provide support and information to those affected by the
Syndrome and to promote knowledge and understanding within
the medical community and public at large.*

ADDIS – The National Attention Deficit Disorder Information and Support Service
P. O. Box 340, Edgware. Middlesex HA8 9HL
Tel: 020 8906 9068. Fax: 020 8959 0727
E-mail: info@addiss.co.uk
Website: www.addis.co.uk
Provides information, training and support for parents, sufferers and professionals in the fields of ADHD and related learning and behavioural difficulties.

Tourette Syndrome (UK) Association
P.O. Box 26149, Dunfermline KY12 9WT
Tel: 08454 581 252. Fax: 01383 629 609
E-mail: enquiries@tsa.org.uk
Website: www.tsa.org.uk
Support and information for parents and carers or children with this condition.

ADULTS

The Basic Skills Agency
Commonwealth House, 1-19 New Oxford Street, London WC1A 1NU
Tel: 020 7405 4017
E-mail: enquiries@basic-skills.co.uk
Website: www.basic-skills.co.uk
The national agency for basic skills in England and Wales.

Skill: The National Bureau for Students with Disabilities
Chapter House, 18-20 Crucifix Lane, London SE1 3JW
Tel: 020 7450 0620. Fax: 020 7450 0650
Helpline: 0800 328 5050
E-mail: info@skill.org.uk
Website: www.skill.org.uk
A voluntary organisation which offers an information service to students with disabilities and/or learning difficulties or people working with them.

Depression Alliance
35 Westminster Bridge Road, London SE1 7JB
Tel: 020 7633 0557. Fax: 020 7633 0559
Helpline: 0845 123 2320
E-mail: information@depressionalliance.org.uk
Website: www.depressionalliance.org.uk

MIND
15-19 Broadway, London E15 4BQ
Tel: 020 8519 2122. Fax: 020 8522 1725
Information Line: 08457 660 163
E-mail: contact@mind.org.uk
Website: www.mind.org.uk
Has material on all aspects of mental health.

The Samaritans
The Upper Mill, Kingston Road, Ewell, Surrey KT17 2AF
Tel: 020 8394 8300. Fax: 020 8394 8301
Helpline: 08457 90 90 90
Helpline: 1850 60 90 90 (Republic of Ireland)
E-mail: admin@samaritans.org
Website: www.samaritans.org.uk
*Has constantly manned telephones in all major towns. See your
local telephone directory.*

Relate (marriage guidance)
Herbert Gray College, Little Church Street, Rugby,
Warwickshire CV21 3AP
Tel: 01788 573 241
Website: www.relate.org.uk
Look in Yellow Pages as well.

Employment Opportunities
58 Newbroad Street, London EC2M 1SL
Tel: 020 7448 5420. Fax: 020 7374 4913
E-mail: info@eopps.org
Website: www.opportunities.org.uk
Helps people with disabilities find suitable employment.

DRIVING ADVICE

MAVIS (Mobility, Advice and Vehicle Information Service)
Crowthorne Business Estate, Macadam Avenue, Old Wokingham
Road, Crowthorne, Berks RG45 6XD
Tel: 01344 661 000. Fax: 01344 661 066
E-mail: mavis@detr.gov.uk
This government organisation helps disabled motorists to make
informed decisions about their mobility needs.

FOR CHILDREN

The Trident Trust
The Smokehouse, Smokehouse Yard, 44046 St John Street,
London EC1M 4DF
Tel: 020 7014 1400. Fax: 020 7336 8561
E-mail: trident@trid.demon.co.uk
Website: www.thetridenttrust.org.uk
Equipping young people with skills for life.

Kidscape
2 Grosvenor Gardens, London SW1W 0DH
Helpline: 020 7730 3300. Fax: 020 7730 7081
E-mail: contact@kidscape.org.uk
Website: www.kidscape.org.uk

Childline
Helpline: 0800 1111 (Open 24 hours a day)
Free national helpline for young people in trouble or danger.

INTERNATIONAL ORGANISATIONS

Canada

The Learning Disabilities Association of Canada (LDAC)
(National Office) 323 Chapel Street, Ottawa, Ontario, Canada
K1N 7Z2
Tel: (613) 238 5712. Fax: (613) 235 539
E-mail: information @ldac-taac.ca
Website: www.ldac.taac.ca

Special Needs Educations Network (Canada)
Website: www.schoolnet.ca

USA

Tourette's Syndrome Association Inc
42-40 Bell Boulevard, Bayside, NY 11361
Tel: (718) 224 2999
Website: www.tsa-usa.org

CHADD (Children and Adults with ADD)
8181 Professional Place, Suite 150, Landover, MD 20785
Tel: (800) 233 4050. Fax: (301) 306 7090
Website: www.chadd.org

ASPEN of America
P. O. Box 2577, Jacksonville, FL 32203-2577
Tel: (904) 745 6741
E-mail: aspen@cybermax.net
Website: www.aspennj.org
*A national organisation for individuals affected by Asperser's
high-functioning autism, semantic pragmatic disorder.*

Index